Marketing Disease to Hispanics

The Selling of Alcohol, Tobacco, and Junk Foods

Bruce Maxwell
Michael Jacobson

Preface by Congressman Matthew G. Martinez
Afterword by Rodolfo Acuña and Juana Mora

Center for Science in the Public Interest   Washington, D.C.

Acknowledgments

We are grateful to the dozens of leaders of Hispanic civic organizations, medical professionals, and researchers who were so generous with their time in providing information for this report. Thanks also to Marilyn Aguirre-Molina, Edmund Benson, Ebenezer Chambi, and Juana Mora for providing videotapes or slides of advertisements.

We especially thank Marilyn Aguirre-Molina, Raul Caetano, Ray Chavira, Carlos Molina, Juana Mora, Pat Taylor, and Rafael Valdivieso for reviewing drafts of this report. Needless to say, the authors are responsible for all interpretations of the data and are solely to blame for any errors.

Finally, this report was supported by grants to CSPI's Action on Minority Health project from the Ruth Mott Fund (Flint, Michigan) and the Henry J. Kaiser Family Foundation (Menlo Park, California), and by donations from CSPI's members.

Center for Science in the Public Interest (CSPI) is a non-profit organization that advocates progressive public health policies. It has led efforts to improve alcohol policies regarding labels and warnings on alcohol beverage containers, advertising, and excise taxes. It also led efforts to eliminate commercials for distilled spirits on Spanish-language television stations.

ISBN: 0-89329-020-3

10 9 8 7 6 5 4 3 2 1

First printing, September 1989

Contents

Tables

(cont.)

Preface

Representative Matthew G. Martinez
U.S. Congress

Amidst all the attention being given to the tremendous strides Hispanics are making in such areas as education, employment, and political empowerment, little notice has been made of another area where Hispanics are closing the gap with Whites: cancer rates.

Historically, cancer rates among Hispanics have been far lower than among Whites. Now, however, that is changing. Today, rates for certain cancers are soaring much faster among Hispanics than Whites, to the point where they now approach — and sometimes surpass — those of the White population.

A national expert quoted in this report calls the skyrocketing Hispanic cancer rates an "epidemic." Scientists attribute the cancer increase primarily to two factors: more Hispanics are smoking, and smokers are smoking more cigarettes than in the past.

The cancer increase strikes a community that is already buffeted by an inordinate rate of problems related to alcoholic beverages. Alcohol abuse previously had been limited almost entirely to men, but today a growing number of Hispanic women are starting to drink as well.

Perhaps more troubling, a handful of studies has found that more Hispanic youths seem to be smoking than ever before, and sometimes in numbers far above their White and Black counterparts.

What causes the drinking and smoking problems in the Hispanic community? Many factors obviously play a role, but one clear contributor is the slick advertising campaigns that alcohol and tobacco companies have aimed at Hispanics for years. The glamorous images in the ads, which are particularly enticing to young people, saturate Hispanic neighborhoods across the country.

Of course, the Hispanic community is not unique in being bombarded with alcohol and tobacco ads. Such advertising pervades our entire society, assaulting every American dozens of times each day from billboards, bus cards, television, magazines, and a host of other sources. Hispanics also are not unique in being specially targeted by the industries, which have aimed similar special advertising campaigns at groups ranging from Blacks to women to blue-collar workers.

In the Hispanic community, as in most of the rest of the country, little is being done to counteract the advertising onslaught. Local groups have undertaken some laudable educational and prevention efforts, but the major national Hispanic organizations have been generally silent about the drinking and smoking problems in their community.

The national groups are subject to great pressure, since many receive tens of thousands of dollars in contributions each year from the alcohol and tobacco industries. These industries have been generous to the Hispanic community (as they have also been to the Black community), providing contributions and sponsoring events while most other companies, foundations, and the federal government have largely ignored Hispanic groups.

Given these circumstances, it's not surprising that the groups feel some gratitude and loyalty toward the alcohol and tobacco companies. Yet as a national Hispanic leader candidly admits in this report, groups that accept contributions do so with the tacit understanding that they will not attack the use of alcohol or tobacco.

To complicate matters further, the fast-food and soft-drink industries are becoming increasingly involved in the Hispanic community, both by sponsoring advertising campaigns and contributing to organizations. The groups this report refers to, however, represent a people who suffer disproportionately from diabetes and obesity: conditions that are aggravated by the calories, fats, and sugars in fast foods and soft drinks. The National Cancer Institute has also implicated fatty foods in the causation of breast and colon cancer.

Some Hispanic groups, such as the Interamerican College of Physicians and Surgeons and the National Association for Chicano Studies, do not take funding from alcohol or tobacco companies. Some other Hispanic groups, in an effort to get away from relying on funds from those companies, are now considering replacing donations from the companies with contributions from their own members. It's much easier to get donations of $10,000 at a time from alcohol and tobacco companies than it is to get 2,000 people to donate $5 each. But the smaller donations could make for a stronger organization and allow Hispanic groups to address the serious — and growing — health problems in the community. This strategy has much merit, although it remains untested.

As important as the issue of whether Hispanic groups should

accept donations from disease-promoting companies, however, is the broader need to start an open dialogue about the role these companies play in the life of the Hispanic community. It is particularly important to look at the pervasive influence of alcohol and tobacco advertising in the community and to explore how it is affecting consumption of booze and cigarettes, especially among youths.

I see these influences reach deeply into my own community every time I walk through areas of my congressional district in California, and I am grateful that a study such as this has been accomplished. This groundbreaking report, with its look at the health, economic, and political issues raised by the activities of the alcohol and tobacco companies, makes an important contribution to the examination that is so badly needed. Not everyone will agree with all its conclusions. There can, however, be little doubt that the issues raised are critical and merit full and vigorous discussion.

FOREWORD

Today, companies are tripping over each other in their excitement about "discovering" the Hispanic market. They're hiring Hispanic ad agencies, advertising in Spanish-language media, and trying to forge ties with the Hispanic community by sponsoring events ranging from festivals to scholarship banquets to soccer games.

But the importance of the Hispanic market is old news for the alcohol and tobacco industries, which targeted Hispanic consumers for extensive — and profitable — advertising and promotional campaigns long before it became the fashionable thing to do.

That targeting is now starting to take its toll. Recent research shows that Hispanics are suffering from an ever-increasing number of health problems related to drinking and smoking. Traditionally, Hispanics have generally had lower rates of drinking and smoking than Whites, but recent studies indicate that Hispanics are catching up and even overtaking Whites in some categories. Most troubling, it appears that Hispanic youths — particularly female teenagers — are becoming increasingly hooked on alcoholic beverages and tobacco.

The alcohol and tobacco companies are now stepping up their efforts to lure Hispanic consumers to become addicted to their products. Drive through any Hispanic neighborhood, and one of the first things you'll notice is a huge number of billboards carrying Spanish-language ads for alcohol or tobacco products. You'll probably also notice, as have numerous researchers, that the concentration of bars and liquor stores is far higher than in comparable White neighborhoods.

Open up a Spanish-language magazine and you'll likely see attractive ads for cigarettes and liquor. Attend a convention of one of the major national Hispanic organizations, and you'll be handed free samples of cigarettes and be able to belly up to a free bar sponsored by a beer company that's open during the entire event.

As if health problems caused by alcohol and tobacco weren't enough, today the fast food and soft drink industries also have targeted Hispanics. Obesity and diabetes rates are much higher in some Hispanic sub-groups than in the general population, and medical problems associated with these conditions will only be exacerbated if the junk-food companies are successful in luring Hispanics to use their products.

This report examines the pervasive influence of the alcohol, tobacco, fast food, and soft drink industries in the Hispanic community and the impact this influence is having on the health of Hispanic people. Unfortunately, very little research exists on the health problems of Hispanics, and what research is available is generally limited to a specific Hispanic sub-group, or a single city. Nevertheless, a growing body of scientific research conclusively documents the seriousness of health problems caused by alcohol and tobacco in the Hispanic community. Even less evidence exists about the impact on Hispanics of eating fatty, sugary foods, but the sketchy information available again indicates a major risk to a significant portion of the Hispanic population.

Two notes on language should be mentioned. Throughout this report, we use the term "Hispanic" to denote people of Mexican, Puerto Rican, Cuban, Central or South American, and Spanish origin. The term "Hispanic" is grossly deficient in describing these diverse peoples, but it seems to be the term that's most widely used. "Hispanic" has certain political connotations for some people, as do other terms such as "Latino." We do not mean to make any political statement by our choice of "Hispanic," but only to use it as a convenient shorthand. In all cases where differences are recorded among Hispanic sub-groups, we clearly define the sub-group being discussed.

Also, because the use of Spanish accent marks varies widely among Hispanic-Americans and organizations, we have omitted all accents from this report.

One final note concerning our motivation in writing this report also is necessary. Some members of the Hispanic community may ask why a largely White organization such as the Center For Science in the Public Interest is concerned about the community's health problems. They may view our efforts as an intrusion, an attempt by outsiders to dictate how the community should respond to its problems.

The Center for Science in the Public Interest has been active in nutrition and alcohol-related issues as they affect the entire society for more than 15 years. Since 1982, CSPI has conducted an extensive investigation into the marketing and advertising practices of the alcoholic beverage industry. Previous reports have included *The Booze Merchants,* which described the aggressive efforts of beer, wine, and liquor producers to maximize sales of their products, and *Marketing Booze to Blacks,* which documented the targeting of the Black population by alcohol producers.

In 1988, CSPI spearheaded a successful drive to persuade Telemundo, the second-largest Spanish-language television network in the United States, to halt the showing of ads for hard liquor. A similar drive earlier persuaded Univision, the largest Spanish-language network, also to halt hard-liquor ads. CSPI cooperated with a number of Hispanic and public health organizations in stopping the ads. CSPI plans to continue cooperating with Hispanic, Black, and other special populations in the future.

The conclusions reached in this report are based on interviews with dozens of people, including national Hispanic leaders, health professionals, scientists, community activists, advertising executives, marketing experts, and industry officials, in addition to an extensive review of the available literature. The key recommendations we make come from the people we interviewed, most of whom are Hispanic. We have acted as reporters, compiling the views of members of the Hispanic community and others who have spent years studying problems that affect the community.

The issue of outside involvement in Hispanic health concerns was probably best addressed by Tony Bonilla, former president of the League of United Latin American Citizens (LULAC), the oldest and largest Hispanic organization in the country. "The problems of Hispanic America are America's problems," said Bonilla, who today is chairman of the National Hispanic Leadership Conference. "The entire population should work diligently with the Hispanic groups to help us address the educational and alcohol and drug abuse problems.

"We've been sitting on our ass reluctant to get other folks to help us. We want to do it with a horse and buggy attitude during a time that we're already traveling to the moon. The bottom line is that we've got to stop being paranoid, we've got to stop being parochial in our views, we must see the broader picture. And that includes embracing people and groups who want to help."[1]

We present this report in the spirit exemplified by Bonilla's remarks, and hope it is received in a like manner.

Bruce Maxwell
Michael Jacobson

Washington, D.C.
August 1989

¿Es verdad
lo que
dicen de
Guinness?

GUINNESS
Morena.
Sugestiva.
Deliciosa.

1

Marketers Discover Hispanics

I n the 1960s, a whole series of ads for the Frito-Lay Corporation featured the "Frito-Bandito," a caricature of a fat, mustachioed Mexican bandit.

The same type of stereotyped image also was used in an ad for Arrid deodorant that showed a gang of banditos riding up in a cloud of dust. The gang's sombrero-bedecked leader halted, reached into his saddle bag for a small object, lifted his arm, and smiled as he sprayed on Arrid. While he did so, an American midwestern voice intoned: "If it works for him, it will work for you."[1]

Such offensive, stereotyped advertising has largely disappeared today. That's not because America's corporations and advertising agencies have suddenly developed a social conscience. Instead, they've simply become aware of the tremendous Hispanic market for goods and services, and they don't want to offend Hispanic consumers.[2]

Perhaps the strongest indication that Hispanics have "arrived" — at least as far as marketers are concerned — occurred during the 1989 Grammy Awards when Pepsi ran an ad entirely in Spanish. The ad starred Puerto Rican teen idol Chayanne, whose songs have topped *Billboard* magazine's Latino charts. Pepsi said it was the first time an all-Spanish ad had ever aired on mainstream television.[3]

Marketers' sudden interest in Hispanics is explained in one word: demographics. The Census Bureau counted 19.4 million Hispanics in March 1988, a whopping 34 percent increase since the 1980 census. Hispanics accounted for 8.1 percent of the total population in 1988,

1

according to the Census Bureau, compared with 6.5 percent in 1980.[4] Many experts believe the Census Bureau severely undercounts Hispanics, and that the nation may actually have as many as 25 million Hispanics.[5]

Even using the conservative Census Bureau figures, from 1980 to 1988 the Hispanic population grew five times faster than the general population, which increased by only seven percent. The annual Hispanic population growth rate is now three percent; the overall growth rate is just 0.9 percent annually. Even during the baby boom of the late 1950s, one of the most dramatic periods for population growth in U.S. history, the annual growth rate was only 1.8 percent.[6]

Of course, generalizations about "Hispanics" ignore the tremendous diversity of the population. The Hispanic population is made up of numerous sub-groups, as Table 1.1 indicates, but Mexican-Americans account for almost two out of three Hispanics.

One of the biggest factors attracting marketers to Hispanics is the youthfulness of the population. The median age for Hispanics in 1988 was 25.5, compared with 32.2 for the general population.[8]

Projections of the Hispanic population in coming years are a marketer's dream. The Hispanic population may double within 20 years and triple within 30, according to Census Bureau projections. A "middle" estimate by the Census Bureau projects 31 million Hispanics by 2010, 47 million in 2040, and 60 million in 2080.[9] However, many experts believe the bureau's projections are low, and the bureau itself says they are conservative. It's projected that Hispanics will surpass Blacks to become the nation's largest minority sometime in the 21st century, although there's little agreement on exactly when the switch will occur.

Hispanic purchasing power also continues to increase. *Hispanic Business* magazine estimates that Hispanic purchasing power will reach $141.6 billion in 1989.[10] All that purchasing power has produced

Table 1.1   Origin of the Hispanic Population in the U.S.

	Millions	Percent
Mexico	12.1	62.3
Puerto Rico	2.5	12.7
Central and South America	2.2	11.5
Cuba	1	5.2
"Other" Hispanic origin	1.6	8.1

Source: U.S. Census Bureau [7]

a lot of breathless prose in articles extolling the virtues of the largely-untapped Hispanic market. "Faster than La Bamba's beat, the USA's advertisers and marketers are creating scripts and strategies to find the buying rhythm of the sizzling Hispanic market," gushed *USA Today*.[11] "Hispanic Markets: Future is Fabuloso," proclaimed a headline in *Adweek*.[12]

A *Business Week* story headlined "Fast Times on Avenida Madison" carried the frenzied subhead: "Advertisers are rushing pell-mell into the Hispanic market — a stunning $130 billion and growing." The article quoted Burton J. Manning, chief executive of J. Walter Thompson Co., the advertising giant, as saying: "No consumer marketer can afford to let this market go. It's not just a matter of growing. It's a matter of surviving." The reporter also hailed the supposed merits of Hispanic consumers: "For companies, these brand-conscious, brand-loyal Hispanics are a blast from a happier past," he wrote. "It's almost as if the last 20 years of erosion of marketing's ability to reach, captivate, and motivate consumers had never happened." To bring the point home, the article quoted a television sales manager who said: "These people haven't been Ralph Naderized."[13]

Hispanics are hit with a double dose of advertising, since they're exposed to mainstream advertising in addition to Spanish-language

Alcohol and tobacco marketers plaster their brand names on everything from conference programs to bus shelters.

ads in the Hispanic media and English ads in publications specifically directed at them. Approximately 250 radio stations and 40 television stations now broadcast at least part-time in Spanish, and about 70 newspapers and an equal number of consumer and business magazines are targeted at Hispanics.[14]

The tremendous interest in the Hispanic market caused *Advertising Age* to start a monthly report on Hispanic marketing in 1987. At the same time, the magazine also doubled to twice a year the frequency of major special sections on marketing to Hispanics. Ironically, while the magazine was boosting its coverage of the Hispanic market, it also was dropping a special section devoted to the Black market. Ed Fitch, managing editor of special sections for the magazine, said the Black section was dropped because of a lack of advertiser interest.[15]

Fitch said demographics are fueling the boom in Hispanic marketing. "It's probably the most attractive minority segment to approach at this point because it's on such a growth curve," he said. Fitch also predicted that the marketing boom will continue. "You will see an increase," he said. "It will level off somewhere, but I think we're at a far distance from that point."

Corporate spending on advertising directed at Hispanics has skyrocketed in recent years, even though it remains a tiny fraction of total advertising expenditures. Spending on Hispanic advertising grew 35 percent in 1983, 27 percent in 1984, 17 percent in 1985, 19 percent in 1986, and 23 percent in 1987, according to figures compiled by *Hispanic Business*.[16] The comparatively small increase of 12.1 percent in 1988 caused the magazine to headline its story "Corporate Ad Spending Takes A Dive," even though expenditures on Hispanic advertising totaled $550.1 million, up from $490.7 million the previous year. In 1988, more than three-quarters of Hispanic advertising dollars

Table 1.2   Hispanic Ad Dollars Spent By Category

Television	45.8%
Radio	32.0
Promotion	9.3
Newspapers and Magazines	9.0
Billboards	3.0
Transit	0.8

Source: *Hispanic Business* [17]

were spent on ads in the electronic media, as shown in Table 1.2.

Some companies caught up by the Hispanic marketing craze have developed sophisticated campaigns to reach Hispanic consumers. A few firms, however, have been burned by embarrassing advertising blunders. Braniff airline's "Fly In Leather" campaign, which was supposed to promote leather airplane seats, was translated into Spanish to "Fly Naked." Chicken-king Frank Perdue didn't fare much better. His theme of "It Takes A Tough Man To Make A Tender Chicken" when translated to Spanish became "It Takes A Sexually-Stimulated Man To Make A Chicken Affectionate."[18]

Even the alcohol and tobacco companies, those pioneers of advertising to Hispanics, have occasionally run into translation problems. Adolph Coors Co. was a victim of translation when an ill-informed copywriter translated the slogan "Turn It Loose" into a phrase that meant "Drink Coors and Get Diarrhea" to one Hispanic subgroup.[19]

Such blunders are rare for alcohol and tobacco companies. Their slick advertising campaigns targeted at Hispanics are usually state-of-the-art and highly successful. Hispanics are now paying the price for that success with an increasing number of health problems, as the next chapter explains.

Para compartir
y saborear.
Winston.

17 mg. "tar", 1.1 mg. nicotine av. per cigarette by FTC method.

Winston
FILTERS

BOX

FULL RICH
TOBACCO TASTE

2

Hispanic Health Risks

S ome hispanic sub-groups suffer from certain diseases — diabetes, liver cirrhosis, and some cancers — at higher rates than the non-Hispanic population.

Drinking heavily, smoking cigarettes, and consuming junk foods can contribute to many of the diseases. Those activities are known in the parlance of health professionals as "risk factors" that increase the likelihood of disease and death. Some of those risk factors are quite prevalent in the Hispanic community, and recent research indicates that others which have been rare in the past are becoming more common.

"...[A]s the population becomes more acculturated, we might anticipate increases in certain risk factors including higher rates of smoking, drinking, and the adoption of a diet more conducive to cardiovascular diseases and certain cancers," concluded researchers at the University of Texas Medical Branch at Galveston.[1]

Traditionally, Hispanics have suffered from many major diseases, such as cancer and heart disease, at lower rates than Whites or Blacks. However, certain Hispanic sub-groups have higher rates than the general population for diseases associated with alcohol abuse, such as cirrhosis of the liver. Hispanics also suffer disproportionately from diabetes, which is aggravated by the calories, fats, and sugars in fast food, candy, and soft drinks.

As Hispanics continue to become more acculturated, researchers expect that their rates for a wide range of diseases will steadily increase. Lung cancer rates among Hispanic men are already

7

starting to skyrocket because of their increased smoking, and cancer rates in general are now increasing much faster among Hispanics than among Whites.

In this chapter, we examine the health problems associated with alcohol abuse, smoking, and consumption of junk foods, and the impact of these health problems on the Hispanic community.

Alcohol

"Clearly, the alcohol problem among the Hispanic American population is so pervasive, so widespread, that it could be labeled an epidemic."[2] Anthony M. Alcocer, a professor of health sciences at California State University at Northridge who has studied Hispanic drinking for more than a decade, wrote those words in 1982. The label "epidemic" still applies today, Alcocer said in a recent interview, at least to the Mexican-American population he continues to study in California.[3]

Other researchers have reached similar conclusions. Alcohol use and dependency "is becoming a major health issue for certain segments of the Mexican-American population," wrote M. Jean Gilbert, scholar in Hispanic alcohol studies at UCLA's Spanish-Speaking Mental Health Research Center. Nearly one-third of older Mexican-American men "can be considered very heavy drinkers," she concluded.[4]

Drinking patterns seem to vary across Hispanic sub-groups, although a lack of hard statistical data continues to hamper researchers. "Not only is there very little research that's been done, but the quality of the early research is very poor," said Patrick Johnson, alcohol research scholar at Fordham University's Hispanic Research Center in New York. "Right now it's kind of like groping in the dark."[5]

"Many studies have been confounded by either too little information, too small a sample size, ambiguous definitions of the term 'Hispanic,' or geographically restrictive information," said an article prepared by the National Institute on Alcohol Abuse and Alcoholism (NIAAA). "Despite these limitations, the data unambiguously suggest that alcohol abuse is a significant health problem in many Hispanic communities."[6]

Dr. Raul Caetano, one of the early pioneers of research into Hispanic drinking, reached the same conclusion in a paper presented to a conference sponsored by the NIAAA. After noting the small amount of research conducted and the difficulty in obtaining hard data, he wrote: "Still, the findings from the various studies have been

Ad agencies assume that the quickest way to a man's wallet is to show a woman's body, as in this poster for Tecate beer and calendar for Budweiser beer. Such ads can be as degrading to men as they are to women.

consistent: When compared to other ethnic groups in the U.S. population, Hispanic men are among the groups with higher rates of heavy drinking and alcohol problems."[7] On the other hand, Caetano found in one study that 52 percent of Hispanic women in northern California drank only occasionally (less than once a month) or not at all, compared to 36 percent of White women.[8]

Virtually no studies have been conducted of drinking by several Hispanic sub-groups. "When people talk about Hispanic drinking in this country, almost all of the research is Mexican-American," said Fordham's Johnson. He added that "at least suggestive evidence" indicates that drinking patterns vary greatly across Hispanic sub-groups.

The Mexican-American sub-group suffers from the greatest alcohol abuse problems, according to the available research. A handful of studies indicates that Puerto Ricans have drinking patterns similar to those of Mexican-Americans. The tiny amount of research available on Cubans shows that they drink significantly less than Mexican-Americans and Puerto Ricans.[9]

One study of those three sub-groups found that Mexican-American men were generally heavier drinkers than Puerto Ricans or Cubans, although Puerto Ricans were close in some categories. For example, 18 percent of Mexican-American men were frequent heavy drinkers, defined as those who drank five or more drinks at a sitting once a week or more often. The corresponding figures for Puerto Ricans and Cubans were 16 percent and five percent, respectively.[10] Even if alcohol abuse is only a serious problem in Mexican-American and Puerto Rican communities, though, it still would affect three-quarters of the U.S. Hispanic population.

The terrible toll that alcohol takes in Mexican-American communities has been well documented for more than a decade. California researchers reported in 1975 that a review of autopsies performed at the Los Angeles County—University of Southern California Medical Center between 1918 and 1970 found that 52 percent of all Mexican-American male deaths between ages 30 and 60 were from alcoholism. For White men, only 24 percent were alcohol-related.[11]

A more recent Texas study found that while the percentage of alcohol-related deaths was the same for Mexican-American men as for Whites, the Mexican-Americans died much earlier. Forty-one percent of Mexican-American men who died from alcohol-related problems succumbed before the age of 50, while only 30 percent of Whites who died from alcohol died so young. And while 72 percent of the Mexican-Americans died before age 60, only 58 percent of White men died before this age. "Given that epidemiologists label deaths occurring before age 64 as 'premature,' these data show that a very large number of Mexican-American men are dying prematurely from causes linked to alcohol," concluded Gilbert in a review of the data.[12]

The *Report of the Secretary's Task Force on Black and Minority Health* found that Mexican-born males have a 40 percent higher risk of death due to cirrhosis than White males. "Cirrhosis is associated with alcohol abuse and suggests that alcohol abuse in Mexican-born males may be a problem," concluded the report by the U.S. Department of Health and Human Services.[13]

Mexican-Americans also have higher rates than the general population of arrests for public drunkenness, arrests for driving while intoxicated, and homicides where the victim was intoxicated.[14] "If the studies reported ... for death rates from cirrhosis of the liver, for public inebriates and drunk driving, and for accidents while drinking and driving are representative of the Hispanic-American population, then it can be concluded that problem drinking is widespread throughout the community," Alcocer wrote.[15]

In states with large Mexican-American populations, the Mexican-Americans utilize alcoholism treatment services in proportions far greater than their representation in the general population.[16] For example, a study by the Texas Commission on Alcoholism found that in 1983–84, Mexican-American males comprised 26 percent of all males in treatment. According to the 1980 U.S. Census, however, their proportion in the Texas population was just under ten percent.[17]

Several disturbing patterns emerge in the drinking practices of Mexican-American men. Although a sizable percentage (20 percent in one study by Caetano) either abstains or drinks very little, another large percentage drinks heavily. In particular, the rate of intoxication-level drinking is higher for Mexican-American men than the general population.

A study in Texas found that of those middle-aged and younger Mexican-American men who drank at least a few times per month, 36.8 percent reported having six or more drinks per occasion. The researchers said the Mexican-American consumption levels "are considerably higher than those observed in the general population."[18]

A survey by Caetano of Hispanics in the San Francisco Bay area, a largely Mexican-American population, found that about 35 percent of the Hispanic men had one or more problems related to alcohol. As indicated in Table 2.1.[19], Hispanics tended to have more alcohol problems than Whites or Blacks.

In addition, while heavy drinking declines in the White population after the 20s, it persists in the Mexican-American population into middle age.[21] "Most men drink fairly heavily in their 20s, and then drop off fairly rapidly," said Gilbert, the scholar in Hispanic alcohol studies at UCLA. "That doesn't happen in the Hispanic population. You see a lot of fathers of teenage boys who are heavy drinkers, so there is a problem of a possible modeling effect."[22] A California study of men age

Table 2.1   Percentage of Men Suffering From Alcohol Problems
(San Francisco Area)

	Hispanic	Black	White
One or more problems	35%	24%	26%
Two or more problems	17	13	13
Three or more problems	12	7	7

Source: Caetano[20]

50 and over found that one-third of the Mexican-American men suffered from alcohol disorder when judged by medical criteria, a rate nearly double that of Whites.[23]

There are nearly as many theories about why Mexican-American men drink heavily as there are researchers who study the problem, and scientific studies sometimes contradict each other. Researchers generally agree, though, that a major factor leading to heavy drinking is the important role that alcohol plays in the Hispanic culture in general and the Mexican-American culture in particular. "Drunkenness seems to be an accepted drinking pattern [among Mexican-Americans], more so than among Whites and Blacks, and as such may contribute to the high prevalence of alcohol problems among Hispanics," Caetano wrote.[24] Table 2.2 indicates that many more Hispanics than Whites or Blacks believe that getting drunk is an innocent, enjoyable thing to do.

Some of the other factors suggested as playing a role in heavy alcohol consumption by Mexican-Americans include low socio-economic status; the difficulty of adjusting to a new culture; discrimination by the majority population; a tradition of heavy drinking in Mexico; targeting of the population by alcohol advertisers; and the

Table 2.2   Attitudes Toward Alcohol Use
(percentage "basically" agreeing with the statement)

	Males			Females		
	Hispanic	Black	White	Hispanic	Black	White
Getting drunk is sometimes a good way to blow off steam	36%	28%	30%	22%	21%	15%
Getting drunk is just an innocent way of having fun	35	28	21	22	18	10
People who drink have more fun than people who don't	21	12	7	13	9	4
People who drink have more friends than people who don't	26	19	8	25	17	6

Source: Caetano[25]

concentrating of liquor outlets in Hispanic neighborhoods at levels up to five times higher than in White neighborhoods.

But researchers really haven't delineated with any precision the factors that are responsible for high drinking rates among Mexican-Americans (or other Hispanic sub-groups). "I think we understand the extent of the problem in the Mexican-American community pretty well," Gilbert said. "What we are lacking is good data on exactly why there is such a high level of alcohol use and drug use."[26]

Traditionally, rates of drinking by Hispanic women have been far lower than those for Hispanic men and for women in the general population, and those who drank generally consumed very little. Caetano found a 32 percent abstinence rate in a sample of Hispanic women in the San Francisco Bay area, compared to 29 percent among Black women and 18 percent among White women. Only 23 percent of Hispanic women fell into Caetano's three heaviest-drinking categories, compared with 29 percent of Black women and 37 percent of White women.[27] A larger national survey of Hispanics by Caetano found a female abstinence rate of 47 percent. The national abstinence rate was much higher than that found in the San Francisco survey, which primarily involved Mexican-American women.[28]

However, increasing evidence suggests that drinking is rising

The elegance and opulence portrayed in ads for liquor and cigarettes contrast sharply with the actual health effects of those products.

among Hispanic women. For example, an analysis across three Mexi-can-American generations in California (see Table 2.3) found significant increases in drinking by the third generation, although the level of drinking was still below that of women in the general population.[29]

A second study across three generations, this one in Texas, also found that drinking among women increased as they became acculturated. "Among younger women, language acculturation is associated with greater frequency of consumption, greater volume, and a higher probability of being a drinker," the researchers wrote.[31]

California researchers determined that certain acculturated Mexican-American women are at risk for developing alcohol problems. "The recent shift of Mexican-American women's drinking from abstaining or occasional use toward heavier drinking suggests that traditional cultural protectors against heavy female alcohol consumption are weakening ... The development of heavier female drinking with acculturation level and expanded opportunities for women indicates that Mexican-American women in higher socioeconomic levels are at risk for developing alcohol-related problems," they wrote.[32] However, Caetano has noted that the heavier drinking has not yet been associated with increased problems.[33]

The drinking problem among Hispanic women may be much more serious than generally believed, according to some researchers, because the women seem to underreport their drinking problems. "Partly because of strong cultural sanctions against female overindulging, Hispanic women may be reluctant to report, even anonymously, problems with alcohol," concluded a report from the National

Table 2.3   Drinking By Mexican-American Women
3 Generations

| | Generation | | |
	First	Second	Third
Drinking frequency			
Almost daily	7%	3%	4%
3-4 week	0	7	7
1-2 week	7	16	19
2-3 month	10	15	23
Once a month or less often	76	59	48

Source: Gilbert and Cervantes[30]

Beer ads are impossible to avoid when watching boxing matches on Spanish-language television.

Institute on Alcohol Abuse and Alcoholism.[34]

The great gender gap between male and female drinking patterns seems to be disappearing among Hispanic youth. "What we're seeing now is not only significantly more drinking at younger ages among Hispanic young people, but the young girls are beginning to drink," said Gilbert.[35]

Peer pressure and parental drinking behaviors seem to be the two biggest factors affecting drinking by youths, Gilbert said. Other researchers say the culture encourages youths to drink. "Mexican-American youth are exposed to values, norms and social environments supporting high consumption of alcohol," wrote Genevieve Ames and Juana Mora, two California researchers. "These cultural and environmental risk factors may be supporting the development of early and problem drinking among male adolescents."[36]

Not surprisingly, heavy alcohol consumption by Hispanic adolescents has been associated with poor performance in school. One study found that of all the Hispanic students who reported a grade average of "D" or "F," 46 percent used alcohol excessively.[37] Of course, a much more detailed study would be required to identify any cause-and-effect relationship between drinking and academic performance.

Tobacco

Traditionally, it's been believed that Hispanics smoked at lower rates than either Blacks or Whites. However, many of the early studies did not break down smoking rates by sex. Researchers now believe that extremely low smoking rates by Hispanic women may have partially masked higher male smoking rates.[38] Most researchers also believe that smoking rates of Hispanic men started increasing in the last few decades, and that female rates started rising more recently.

"...[A] review of recent surveys suggests that prevalence among Hispanic males is as high as that of non-minority males," said the *Report of the Secretary's Task Force on Black and Minority Health.* "Also, recent marketing efforts in the Southwest aimed at encouraging tobacco use may result in increased smoking among Hispanics."[39] Table 2.4 compares smoking rates among Hispanics, Blacks, and Whites. The table indicates that Hispanic women tend to smoke considerably less than Blacks or Whites, whereas Hispanic men tend to smoke at about the same rate as other men.

Data from the 1982–83 Hispanic Health and Nutrition Examination Survey (HHANES), the most comprehensive survey of Hispanic health in recent years, show that smoking rates among Hispanic men are nearly identical across the major sub-groups. The study found that 43.6 percent of Mexican-American men were smokers, as were 41.8 percent of Cuban men and 41.3 percent of Puerto Rican men.

The results for women were more mixed. Some 32.6 percent of Puerto Rican women smoked, compared with 24.5 percent of Mexican-American women and 23.1 percent of Cubans.

The campaign that started in 1964 to convince Americans to stop smoking has had a much larger impact on the general population than

Table 2.4   Smoking Rates of Hispanics, Blacks, and Whites

	Hispanics	Blacks	Whites
National Health Interview Survey, 1980[40]			
Males	38.4%	42.0%	35.7%
Females	21.1	30.0	29.7
Polls by Louis Harris & Associates[41]			
1983:			
Males and females	28	36	29
1987:			
Males and females	30	29	28
National Behavioral Risk Factor Surveys, 1981 to 1983[42]			
Males	34.8	35.0	34.1
Females	16.7	25.0	30.1

on Hispanics, wrote researchers who studied the HHANES data. "The previous two decades' passive and active campaigns aimed at curbing cigarette smoking among the public in general appeared to have had some impact on the smoking habits of Mexican-American men," the researchers wrote. "No comparable improvements were apparent in the smoking patterns of other Hispanic men and women; cigarette smoking actually became more prevalent among Cuban-American and Puerto Rican-American women."[43]

As Table 2.4 indicates, Hispanic women in the past have smoked at rates far below those of their White and Black counterparts. But researchers say acculturation is causing an increase in smoking by female Hispanics. "Almost exclusively Hispanic women have been non-smokers until very recently, the mid-1980s or so, when younger women have started taking up smoking," said Felipe Castro, associate professor in the Graduate School of Public Health at San Diego State University. "The pattern appears to be that younger Hispanic females are smoking more than the previous cohort. A lot has to do with level of acculturation, how traditional the person is versus how non-traditional or acculturated to the American scene."[44]

While Hispanic women have just recently started to smoke more, the beginning of the increase in smoking by Hispanic men can be traced back at least a couple of decades. Evidence of the increased male smoking is turning up today in escalating rates of lung cancer among Hispanic men. "There is a big increase in lung cancer rates among Hispanic males, and 85 percent of all lung cancer in this country has been attributed to smoking," said Al Marcus, a cancer specialist at UCLA's Jonsson Comprehensive Cancer Center. "So that's happening right now."

Marcus said a study he conducted of lung cancer rates found "tremendous increases in cancer incidence (among Hispanics) compared to White Anglos." The study covered Hispanic populations in Los Angeles, New Mexico, Denver, and Puerto Rico. Most of the increases in cancer rates were linked to tobacco or diet, he said.

"There's an epidemic out there," Marcus said. "And it hasn't received a lot of attention." Why not? "There aren't a lot of people studying cancer among Hispanics."[45]

Several studies have documented a rising lung cancer rate among Hispanic males. For example, the Colorado Tumor Registry reported a 132 percent increase in lung-cancer rates among Hispanic males between 1970 and 1980, compared to only a 12 percent increase among White males.[46]

Table 2.5   Lung Cancer Rates for Hispanics and Whites
(age-adjusted lung cancer rates per 100,000
person-years, Denver area)

	1969-71		1979-81	
	Hispanics	**Whites**	**Hispanics**	**Whites**
Males	23.1	57.0	45.6	68.9
Females	8.1	11.6	16.9	22.6

Source: Savitz[47]

A Denver study covering roughly the same time period also documented an approximate doubling of lung-cancer rates in both Hispanic males and females (see Table 2.5). Hispanic male lung-cancer rates increased by 97 percent over the ten-year study period, compared to a 21 percent increase for White males. Lung cancer among Hispanic females grew by 109 percent, compared with 95 percent for White females.

In New Mexico, deaths from lung cancer nearly tripled for Hispanic males from 1958 to 1982, while only doubling for White males (see Table 2.6). In addition, the Hispanic male death rate from chronic obstructive pulmonary disease, a respiratory disease related to smoking, grew six-fold over the period, while the comparable White rate increased less than four-fold.

Table 2.6   Mortality Rates for Smoking-Related Diseases
(Age-adjusted mortality rates [per 100,000 persons] for lung cancer and chronic obstructive pulmonary disease among New Mexico Hispanic and White males).

Cause of Death	1958-62	1963-67	1968-72	1973-77	1978-82
Lung Cancer					
Hispanics	10.1	14.5	18.2	20.1	28.8
Whites	30.1	34.6	48.3	56.6	62.9
Chronic Obstructive Pulmonary Disease					
Hispanics	5.0	11.4	13.0	20.6	30.1
Whites	17.0	41.8	48.0	56.3	64.5

Source: Samet, Wiggins, Key, and Becker[48]

In an article reporting the New Mexico lung cancer data, the researchers wrote that the "strong trends of increasing mortality from lung cancer and from chronic obstructive pulmonary disease across the study period imply increasing smoking by Hispanic males."

The researchers wrote that they expected the increase in Hispanic lung cancer rates to continue. "The tobacco industry has targeted advertising at the Hispanic population of the United States," they wrote. "Success of such advertising will accelerate the trends that we have documented through 1982."[49]

The cancer epidemic among Hispanics will get worse in the future because there's typically a 20-year incubation period between the onset of smoking and development of cancer, Marcus said. In a 1984 paper reporting his research, he wrote: "...[R]ates of Hispanic lung cancer (and other cigarette-linked diseases) *may increase sharply within this decade, and continue to increase into the next century.* This hypothesis is based on the assumption that the lower rate of lung cancer among Hispanics of today reflects a period in time when Hispanics smoked less frequently than White/Anglos. However, current evidence suggests that Hispanic males are now smoking as frequently as their White/Anglo counterparts" (emphasis in original).[50]

Dr. John Samet of the University of New Mexico School of Medicine, one of the researchers who documented the increasing lung-cancer rates in Hispanic males in New Mexico, said the higher rates are occurring because Hispanic men have started smoking more cigarettes in the last ten to 15 years. In the past, Hispanic smokers smoked far fewer cigarettes per day than their White or Black counterparts. One study, for example, found that Mexican-American males and females smoked about one-half a pack fewer cigarettes per day than Whites.[51] However, that now seems to be changing.

"The disease risks have been quite low for cigarette-related diseases in the Hispanic population in New Mexico," Samet said. "But it's clear that picture is changing in the males. Lung cancer rates are rising rather steeply, over the last 20 years or so, as are the rates for chronic obstructive pulmonary disease." What will the future likely hold? "I think we should look to further increases in cigarette-related diseases in Hispanic males," Samet said.[52]

A three-generation study of smoking among Mexican-Americans in San Antonio, Texas, also predicted an increase in Hispanic cancer rates. "...[O]ur findings clearly indicate that smoking rates among Mexican-Americans in San Antonio are high, particularly among men," the researchers reported. "It is also likely that these high smoking rates will translate into rising rates of cancer and other smoking-related diseases in the near future."[53]

In addition to lung cancer, tobacco also causes mouth, throat, bladder, and other cancers. "It is apparent that tobacco use (cigarettes and smokeless) contributes significantly to the excess incidence, morbidity, and mortality experienced by U.S. minority groups compared to the general population," wrote Dr. Claudia Baquet, a specialist in minority cancer with the National Cancer Institute. "The adverse health effects of tobacco are even more striking when the synergistic effects of occupational exposures or alcohol are taken into consideration."[54] Thus, the increased smoking rate of Hispanic men, coupled with their high rate of heavy drinking, places them at especially high risk for developing mouth and throat cancers. And as Hispanic women continue to drink and smoke more heavily, their cancer risk also jumps.

Hispanics already suffer from certain types of cancers linked to smoking at rates far higher than those for Blacks and Whites, according to data compiled for the *Report of the Secretary's Task Force on Black and Minority Health.* For example, the incidence of stomach cancer in Hispanics is twice that of non-minorities. The development of stomach cancer has been correlated to smoking and diets high in smoked, pickled, and spiced foods.[55]

In addition, the incidence of esophageal cancer is 20 percent higher among Hispanic females in New Mexico than among non-minority females. "Studies suggest a link between the development of esophageal cancer and smoking and alcohol consumption with these two having a synergistic effect," said the task force report. Other possible risk factors included poor nutrition and drinking hot beverages. Hispanics in New Mexico also have rates of cancer of the pancreas, which is linked to smoking, that are higher than those of non-minorities.[56]

The Denver study referred to earlier that found dramatic increases in Hispanic lung cancer rates also found major increases in overall cancer rates (see Table 2.7). The male Hispanic cancer rate rose 52 percent during the ten-year period studied, compared to 12 percent for White males. Even more striking was the jump in the overall cancer rate for Hispanic females, an increase of 77 percent in just 10 years. The corresponding increase for White women was ten percent. Whereas at the beginning of the study period Hispanic women had cancer rates significantly below White women, by the end of the study period their cancer rate had slightly eclipsed that of White women.

Perhaps the biggest concern now is the high rate of smoking among Hispanic youths. "The initiation of smoking among young adolescents seems to be much higher among Hispanic kids than either Whites or Blacks," said Marcus of UCLA. "That's a particularly disturbing problem."[58]

One of the few studies ever conducted of smoking among Hispanic youths found consistently higher "ever smoked" and "currently" smoke rates for Hispanic children than for either Black or White children. The study of fourth- and fifth-grade students, conducted as part of the Los Angeles "Know Your Body" program, found that 13.1 percent of the Hispanic boys said they had smoked a cigarette, compared with 9.3 percent of Blacks and 6.7 percent of Whites. Some 5.3 percent of Hispanic boys reported that they currently smoked, compared to 3.5 percent of Blacks and 0.8 percent of Whites. Among girls, 1.6 percent of Hispanics said they currently smoked, compared with 1.1 percent of Blacks and 0.9 percent of Whites.[59]

A study in the early 1980s of Mexican-American youths found that 28.9 percent smoked, compared with 19.1 percent of Whites and 15.2 percent of Blacks.[60]

A survey in Albuquerque, New Mexico, of children aged 10 to 15 found slightly lower rates of never having smoked among Hispanics than among Whites, as shown in Table 2.8. The researchers concluded: "Our survey findings imply that an increasing burden of cigarette-related morbidity and mortality in southwestern Hispanics will manifest itself unless effective interventions are implemented ... Adolescent smoking strongly predicts smoking in adulthood."[61]

Table 2.7   Overall Cancer Rates Among Hispanics and Whites
(age-adjusted rates per 100,000 person-years for
15 different cancers, Denver area)

	1969-71		1979-81	
	Hispanics	Whites	Hispanics	Whites
Males	212.7	335.8	323.7	377.7
Females	166.7	266.1	294.7	292.6

Source: Savitz[57]

Hip billboards (and magazine ads) touting Camel cigarettes are designed to attract youthful eyes.

A study published in early 1989, based on data collected as part of the Hispanic Health and Nutrition Examination Survey, found smoking rates for youths aged 13 to 19 were significantly higher among Puerto Ricans than among their Mexican-American and Cuban counterparts. Some 21.7 percent of the Puerto Rican male youths smoked, according to the study, as did 19.1 percent of Puerto Rican females. Among Mexican-American teens, the smoking rates were 12.9

Table 2.8   Cigarette Use by Hispanic and White Children, Aged 10-15
(Albuquerque, New Mexico)

	Males		Female	
	Hispanic	White	Hispanic	White
Current	10.8%	12.0%	16.1%	15.0%
Experimental	31.1	27.9	40.4	34.1
Never	58.1	60.1	43.5	50.9

Source: Greenberg, Wiggins, Kutvirt, and Samet[62]

percent for boys and 7.9 percent for girls, while the rates for Cuban teens were 7.9 percent for boys and 8.1 percent for girls.[63]

Early smoking places the youths at increased risk for coronary heart disease (CHD), according to a study conducted by Castro and his colleagues at UCLA. "... [I]t would appear that (Hispanic) adolescent males, and to a lesser extent adolescent females, are at a higher risk of eventually developing CHD based upon smoking rates, when contrasted with their same-sex peers," they wrote. "Should these trends be confirmed by future research, then immediate preventive interventions will be required to reduce the apparent increasing rate of smoking among young Hispanics."[64]

Diet

It's easy to avoid health problems related to alcohol and tobacco simply by drinking sparingly and not smoking. However, diet-related health problems are tougher to avoid, because we all must eat. Diets high in fat, cholesterol, sodium, and sugar contribute to obesity, diabetes, heart disease, tooth decay, high blood pressure, and probably certain cancers. Data on disease rates among Hispanics are rather skimpy, but it is clear that diabetes and obesity are particularly common.

Diabetes kills a total of 36,000 people each year and contributes to another 95,000 deaths in the United States.[65] Research has shown that diabetics, and overweight people who have a family history of diabetes, should cut down on calories, especially from fat,[66][67] and eat less sugar.[68]

According to the national Hispanic Health and Nutrition Examination Survey, diabetes strikes 26.1 percent of Puerto Ricans, 23.9 percent of Mexican-Americans, and 15.8 percent of Cuban-Americans aged 45 to 74. Rates for the same age group are 12 percent for Whites and 19.3 percent for Blacks.[69]

A survey of Hispanics, primarily Mexican-Americans, in the Southwest found that prevalence and mortality rates for noninsulin-dependent (Type II, adult-onset) diabetes were two to five times greater than those found in the general U.S. population.[70]

Diabetes can adversely affect the eyes, kidneys, nerves, heart, and blood vessels. Diabetics are two and one-half times more likely to die from complications of the disease than from the disease itself. In diabetics over 20 years old, kidney disease is responsible for nearly half of the extra deaths, with most of the remaining deaths due to

Ads on Spanish-language television for candy bars and sugary breakfast cereals do nothing to reduce the prevalence of obesity and diabetes among Hispanics.

heart disease.[71] "...[M]ortality statistics for diabetes greatly underestimate the true impact of this disease on overall mortality in the U.S.," concluded the *Report of the Secretary's Task Force on Black and Minority Health.*[72]

The U.S. Surgeon General has found that obesity "is strongly associated with the onset and severity of Type II diabetes."[73] At least 80 percent of people with Type II diabetes are more than 15 percent overweight. Some scientists have suggested that new cases of diabetes could be cut in half if obesity were prevented in middle-aged adults.[74] The U.S. National Diabetes Commission reported that the risk of becoming diabetic more than doubles with every 20 percent increase in weight above normal.[75]

Studies show that it's not only how fat a person is that matters, but how long that person has been fat[76] and where the extra fat is carried. For example, people who carry more fat on their chest and abdomen than on their hips and thighs are more likely to develop Type II diabetes.[77] Recent data from the San Antonio Heart Study confirmed that Mexican-American women who carried their weight on their upper bodies were at greater risk.[78]

Mexican-Americans suffer from obesity at rates higher than the U.S. average.[79] "Available evidence indicates that obesity is a major problem in Mexican-Americans, especially among women and those of low socioeconomic status," said the *Report of the Secretary's Task Force on Black and Minority Health.*[80] The 1985 National Health Interview Survey found that Hispanic women suffered from obesity at rates higher than White women, as shown in Table 2.9.

Many of the dietary recommendations for treating diabetes are

Table 2.9   Obesity Among Women Aged 18 and Over
(percentages, standardized for age and poverty status)

	Hispanic	Black	White
Relative Weight			
10-19.9% above ideal	15.6%	15.7%	12.2%
20% or more above ideal (obese)	25.5	34.7	20.2

Source: Dawson[81]

the same as those made for treating heart disease, said Dr. Michael Stern, professor of medicine at the University of Texas Health Science Center in San Antonio and author of the paper on Hispanic diabetes in the task force report. "There's a big overlap with heart issues, because one of the reasons for dietary treatment of diabetics is to prevent heart disease, which is the main complication," he said. Avoiding saturated fats and cholesterol "is doubly important if you're a diabetic," Stern said.

People with diabetes have higher blood cholesterol and triglyceride levels and lower levels of "good" HDL cholesterol than non-diabetics[82] and are two to four times more likely to have heart disease.[83] The first approach for normalizing those blood fats is to reduce high blood-sugar levels; this will frequently increase the "good" HDL cholesterol and decrease triglyceride levels.[84] Weight loss through calorie restriction is the most effective method for lowering blood-sugar levels, and has the added advantage of lowering "bad" LDL cholesterol and triglyceride levels as well.[85]

A diet containing 50 to 60 percent of total calories as carbohydrates is recommended for people with diabetes,[86] not only because high-carbohydrate diets improve blood-sugar levels,[87] but also because the reduced level of fat, especially saturated fat, that accompanies a high-carbohydrate diet lowers the "bad" LDL cholesterol and decreases the risk of heart disease. Eating carbohydrates instead of fat also should substantially cut calories, because fat has twice as many calories per gram as do carbohydrates.

Most fast food is loaded with fat and cholesterol. Fast food hamburgers typically contain five to 15 teaspoons of fat, according to industry data. "We have a saying about the McDonald's arches: If you go through them, you go faster to the pearly gates," said Dr. Mariano Garcia, chairman of the American Diabetes Association's minority task force in Florida.[88]

Diabetics also should avoid drinking regular soft drinks unless their sugar levels are low, Garcia said. The National Institutes of Health has concluded that sugar intake up to five percent of carbohydrate calories (about three teaspoons per day) is okay in diabetics who are lean and have normal triglyceride levels.[89] But that's fewer than one out of five diabetics. (For sake of comparison, one regular can of cola contains about ten teaspoons of sugar.) Diabetics can drink diet soft drinks, which do not contain any sugar.

Surveys indicate that Hispanics consume more fast food and cola soft drinks than other groups. For example, Hispanics in San Antonio spend 36 percent more at fast-food restaurants than other groups, and account for 65 percent of sales of sugared colas even though they make up only 54 percent of the population, according to the ad agency Sosa & Associates.[90] A survey in Los Angeles found that McDonald's was even more popular among Hispanics than among non-Hispanics. Moreover, Hispanic consumers averaged one-third more visits per month to fast-food restaurants than non-Hispanics (12 versus nine).[91] Coca-Cola's director of Hispanic consumer markets was quoted as saying that Hispanics account for more than $2 billion in soft drink sales annually.[92]

Garcia said it's unknown exactly what proportion of diabetic problems are tied to diet, "but you can assume it's the main problem." However, many diabetics aren't aware they should control their diets because they don't know they have the disease. About half the people, both Hispanic and non-Hispanic, who meet the criteria for having diabetes don't know they have the disease, Stern said. Thus, Hispanic diabetics who aren't aware they have the disease may be unwittingly contributing to the seriousness of their condition by continuing to consume fast food and soft drinks.

Hispanics also have higher rates than non-Hispanics of certain other diseases that can be affected by diet. For example, Hispanic women seem to be slightly more vulnerable than White women to hypertensive disease and strokes, and Mexican-American men have higher hypertension rates than White males. However, extremely limited research seems to indicate that Hispanics in general suffer from coronary heart disease at rates lower than Whites.[93]

The high rates of death and disease related to alcohol, tobacco, fast foods, and soft drinks in the Hispanic community have not slowed down companies that produce and market those products. Instead, the companies have stepped up their campaigns to hook Hispanic consumers, as we shall see in the next chapter.

3

Targeting Hispanics

F or years, alcohol and tobacco companies have targeted Hispanics with major advertising campaigns. "They are some of
the bigger players in this area," said Ed Fitch, a managing editor
at *Advertising Age* who specializes in reporting about Hispanic marketing.

"They're smart marketers, and they're always quick to spot an
opportunity," Fitch said. "Regardless of what you think of them, they
sure know how to sell products."[1]

Indeed they do. Today, the Hispanic community is paying the
price for the marketing savvy of the alcohol and tobacco companies
with increased levels of drinking and smoking. The increases are
particularly apparent among Hispanic women, who have been specially targeted by the alcohol and tobacco companies because of their
traditionally low rates of drinking and smoking, and young people.

Officials of the alcohol and tobacco industries vehemently deny
they've targeted Hispanics. "Anti-smoking groups make this allegation (about targeting) as one of the rounds of ammunition they try to
come up with in terms of looking for ad-ban legislation or ad-restric-
tion legislation," said Gary Miller, assistant to the president of the
Tobacco Institute, the industry lobbying group. "Their allegation is
that (companies are) trying to recruit smokers among these ranks.
Now, really what it is is that through just typical marketing research,
just as with any particular product, cigarette companies have found
that these people, Blacks and Hispanics, enjoy smoking. There's a
large percentage of smokers in these groups, so let's get our message
to them."[2]

As we shall see, the connection between the targeting of Hispanics by tobacco and alcohol companies and increased smoking and

Table 3.1   Top Advertisers in the Hispanic Market, 1988

Rank	Company	Hispanic ad spending (in millions)
1	Procter & Gamble Co.	$20.8
2	Philip Morris Cos.	13.1
3	Anheuser-Busch Co.	8.6
4	Colgate-Palmolive Co.	7.9
5	McDonald's Corp.	6.6
6	Adolph Coors Co.	5.1
7	Johnson & Johnson	4.9
8	Ford Motor Co.	4.1
9	Kraft Inc.	3.7
10	Sears, Roebuck & Co.	3.4
15	PepsiCo Inc.	2.9
25	Coca-Cola Co.	1.6

Source: *Hispanic Business*[3]

drinking seems too clear to dispute. The alcohol and tobacco companies like to claim there's no connection, that they advertise not to hook new drinkers and smokers but only to preserve their market share and to steal market share from other brands. But these industries are killing off some of their best customers, and must have new customers to survive.

The targeting of Hispanics by disease-promoting companies, including fast-food and soft-drink firms, is apparent in the annual list compiled by *Hispanic Business* of the top advertisers in Hispanic media (see Table 3.1). In 1988, four of the top six advertisers were disease-promoting companies. These included Philip Morris (cigarettes, coffee, frozen foods, Miller beer, Oscar Mayer hot dogs, Post cereals), Anheuser-Busch (beer), McDonald's (hamburgers, french fries), and Adolph Coors (beer). The soft drink companies PepsiCo and Coca-Cola placed 15th and 25th, respectively. The biggest advertiser, Procter & Gamble, sells a wide variety of soaps, toothpastes, and such fatty foods as Pringles potato chips, Crisco shortening and oil, and Jif peanut butter.

In this chapter, we examine how the alcohol, tobacco, fast-food, and soft-drink industries have targeted advertising to Hispanics.

Alcohol

The 1960s may have been the decade for Black achievement, but the 1980s are "The Decade of the Hispanic," according to a slogan popular in the community.

Sexy women on billboards push "high-octane" Olde English "800" and other malt liquors in Hispanic communities, fueling the high rate of alcohol problems among Hispanic men.

One might think such a slogan was coined by a Hispanic organization. It wasn't. Instead, it was created as part of an advertising campaign by the Adolph Coors Co., a beer brewer whose relationship with Hispanics has been rocky at best. The Hispanic magazine *Nuestro* said it was "a sad irony" that the slogan was conceived by Coors "in order to sell more beer."[4]

The Coors example makes it clear that alcohol companies have no shame when it comes to trying to hook Hispanics on their products. That lack of shame is exemplified by an advertising campaign for Olde English "800" malt liquor, which is manufactured by the Pabst Brewing Co. Malt liquor is similar to beer, but has 10 to 50 percent more alcohol.

In the billboard version of the ad, a buxom Hispanic woman wearing a string bikini crouches on the beach next to a tiger. Superimposed on the scene is a picture of a can of Olde English "800" malt liquor and the slogan in Spanish: "It's the Power."

In promotional materials sent to liquor retailers, the brewer says billboards featuring the "Lady and the Tiger" design are "strategically placed in ethnic neighborhoods," and radio and television ads with the same theme are being run "in all major Ethnic markets." Why would Olde English "800" appeal to ethnic people? "More emphasis on taste — its smooth, mellow taste brewed for relatively high alcohol content (important to the Ethnic market!)," according to the promotional materials.

The cynicism underlying the campaign is clear, as is the message in the ads relating heavy drinking to sexual conquest. However, other brewers are following Pabst's lead in targeting Hispanics with malt liquor. In March 1989, the G. Heileman Brewing Co. announced it was rolling out a dry malt brew called Colt 45 Dry, which it planned to aim at Hispanic and Black drinkers.[5]

The Olde English "800" ad campaign may be the most offensive effort aimed at Hispanics by an alcohol company, although there are many other alcohol campaigns strongly competing for that dubious honor.

A series of huge billboards placed in California Hispanic neighborhoods showed six bottles of Corona beer serving as "pillars" for an ornate building that could easily be a government center. "Pillars of Society," read the inscription underneath.

When one of the billboards appeared in Los Angeles County, Dr. Ebenezer Chambi, Ray Chavira, and a group of people who came primarily from the Seventh Day Adventist Church decided to take action. "We felt it was kind of like a slap in the face," said Chavira, a community activist and board member of the California Council on Alcohol Problems. "Now that they're pushing [Corona beer] a lot all over the place, they have the audacity to tell us that it's a pillar of society. What could be further from the truth?"

To protest the signs, Chambi, Chavira, and the group organized a sidewalk demonstration outside the Los Angeles County Hall of Ad-

Ray Chavira and Ebenezer Chambi succeeded in eliminating billboards in southern California that indicated that Corona beer bottles were the pillars of Mexican-American society.

ministration and met with the Board of Supervisors' staff. Television and newspaper reporters from both the general and Spanish-language media covered their protest. The board chairman complained to a top official of Gannett Outdoor Advertising, which owned the billboard, and another supervisor wrote a letter to Gannett protesting the sign. "Within days, the Corona sign was taken down," Chavira said. Identical billboards in other parts of the state also were removed.

Chavira said there's an important lesson to be learned from the experience of his citizens' group: "Big companies and big and powerful politicians do have a conscience and they do listen, because every little bit of bad p.r. and bad publicity hurts their profits."[6]

Most of the time, though, the ads go unchallenged no matter how offensive. A series of billboards and subway posters sponsored by Glenmore Distilleries, a liquor distributor in the Northeast, exploited the use of wine in Catholic ceremony. The Spanish-language ad showed a priest and a monk gazing toward a light shining from above while holding glasses of Felipe II brandy. Translated, the copy read: "To drink it is not a sin."[7]

Marilyn Aguirre-Molina, assistant professor at the University of Medicine and Dentistry of New Jersey, said the Felipe ad was "one of the most appalling ads" she's seen in recent years. It played off the Hispanic culture's respect for the Catholic church, and Aguirre-Molina said many of the alcohol ads focus on aspects of the Hispanic culture.

"The one thing that they have focused on in the Latino market is really understanding the cultural nuances of family, friends, and drinking patterns, and they've really managed to capture that dynamic in their advertising," she said. "They know something about drinking patterns among Latinos. They know more about our culture than I think health service providers know."[8]

The use of cultural themes is an attempt to legitimize the use of alcohol, which is already pervasive in the Hispanic culture. The targeting of alcohol advertising to Hispanics "simply expands the favorable climate toward alcohol use," said M. Jean Gilbert, scholar in Hispanic alcohol studies at UCLA's Chicano Studies Research Center.[9] Many of the ads are tied into Hispanic celebrations such as Mexican Independence Day and Cinco de Mayo.[10]

Billboards advertising alcohol are ubiquitous in most Hispanic neighborhoods across the country. "It's obvious when you drive around the Hispanic areas of San Antonio or Los Angeles that there are more and more billboards advertising alcohol products with

Billboards pushing alcohol and tobacco clutter East Los Angeles and other Hispanic communities. Many parents are angry that these ads encourage their children to adopt a pathogenic lifestyle.

Hispanic faces on them," said Dr. Kyriakos Markides, professor of preventive medicine and community health at the University of Texas Medical Branch in Galveston.[11] Merrill Singer, director of research at the Hispanic Health Council in Hartford, Conn., said there are a "noticeable number" of billboards advertising alcohol in the Puerto Rican community he serves.[12]

Since the 1970s, the alcohol industry has been the second leading advertiser on billboards behind the tobacco industry, according to Scenic America, the nation's leading anti-billboard organization. The billboard industry has saturated low-income neighborhoods, particularly Hispanic and Black areas, with thousands of new signs advertising tobacco and alcoholic beverages. "A much higher percentage of billboards in ethnic neighborhoods advertise alcohol and liquor products compared to billboards in other areas," according to the coalition.[13]

The beer industry also advertises heavily on Spanish-language radio and television stations. "We are definitely seeing an increase in the number of beer commercials that have dancing Hispanics on TV," said Jane Garcia, executive director of La Clinica de la Raza in

Oakland, Calif. Garcia said she's troubled by the commercials. "When you have these visions of it being such a fun time and there are no health ramifications to it, then it sure makes it attractive," she said.[14]

Many of the beer commercials feature Hispanic sports figures and other personalities as spokesmen. For example, an ad for Miller Lite beer showed former welterweight champ Carlos Palomino sitting in a bar surrounded by friends. "Y'know, one of the best things about coming to America was that I got to try American beers," Palomino said in the ad. "I tried them all. And the one I like best is Lite Beer from Miller."[15] Miller has also used other Hispanics such as ex-Oakland Raider Ben Davidson, an ex-bullfighter, and Paul Rodriguez, star of the ill-fated television series "a.k.a. Pablo."[16]

One of the most popular advertising vehicles on Spanish-language television is the hit show Sabado Gigante (Giant Saturday), a raucous blend of music, skits, talk, and out-and-out huckstering that runs for three and a half hours each Saturday night on the Univision network. "The show is a marketer's dream," says Business Week.

Sabado Gigante *(Univision network) is an advertiser's delight. Brand names are shown on-screen for minutes at a time. Don Francisco and his co-host exhort viewers to drink Coors beer.*

"Brands such as Coca-Cola and Coors are openly pitched during the program, their names repeated dozens of times."[17]

The show's host, don Francisco, even leads the audience in singing advertising jingles for products that sponsor the program. And the viewership numbers are unbelievable: Some 47 percent of all U.S. Hispanic households watched the show in February 1988. The Cosby Show, by comparison, was only watched by a comparatively paltry 27.8 percent of all U.S. households during an average week of the 1987–88 season.[18]

Until 1987, hard liquor was advertised regularly on Spanish-language television. English-language radio and television stations rarely accept ads for distilled spirits, under a longstanding voluntary agreement among broadcasters and liquor companies. However, the Spanish-language stations accepted the ads until a coalition of public health and Hispanic organizations pressured the two Spanish-language television networks to stop the practice.

Univision, the largest Spanish-language television network, stopped accepting ads for hard liquor in late 1987, and Telemundo dropped most of its ads as of January 1, 1989 (it said it had a commitment to run Bailey's Irish Cream ads in 1989).[19] Organizations involved in the campaign to get the liquor ads pulled included the Center for Science in the Public Interest, California state PTA leaders, National Council on Alcoholism, Doctors Ought to Care (DOC), Latino Caucus of the American Public Health Association, LULAC Foundation, Community Service Organization of California, El Congreso Nacional de Asuntos Colegiales, and National Coalition of Hispanic Health and Human Services Organizations (COSSMHO).

The Spanish-language television stations have been able to do without the modest amount of lost advertising, but some observers believe that some Hispanic newspapers and magazines would shrink in size, or even fold, without advertising from the alcohol and tobacco industries. "Without these two core advertising groups, their margin of profit would be cut pretty slim, and I think you would probably see some of these publications go out of business," said Ed Fitch, the *Advertising Age* editor who specializes in Hispanic marketing.[20]

Jerry Apodaca, the former publisher of *Hispanic* magazine, agreed with Fitch. "If we had done away with the tobacco and beer ads, we'd have been in serious trouble," he said.[21]

In 1988, the National Association of Hispanic Publications gave Philip Morris (Marlboro cigarettes, Miller beer) its company-of-the-year award, showing once again the close link between Hispanic

Univision and Telemundo, the major Spanish-language networks, bowed to public pressure and stopped carrying ads for hard liquor, which is not advertised on English-language television. Public-service ads are as rare on these networks as on NBC, CBS, and ABC.

publications and the alcohol and tobacco industries.

That link is apparent in reading most Hispanic publications. For example, the March 1989 issue of *Hispanic* — one of the leading magazines for Hispanics — featured a full-page article on the creation of a world-record, 119,000-person conga line at Miami's Calle Ocho Festival in March 1988. The article, while a year out of date, prominently featured comments from Scott Fortini, identified as "a representative of Guinness Stout." He apparently was quoted because the conga line was going to be listed in *The Guinness Book of World Records.* But a major section of the article was devoted to helping Fortini push Guinness Stout:

> The Hispanic community treasures a long relationship with foreign beers, said Fortini. "Guinness has a very loyal Latin following," he said. "The Cuban and Latin market has traditionally very loyal Guinness drinkers (sic)." Foreign beers such as Guinness have always been widely available in the homelands of many Hispanics. Thus, they still drink it in the United States, because their parents drank it, and they like "prestigious" brands, Fortini said. "They're very image-conscious."[22]

Within less than 30 pages, readers came across a full-page ad for Guinness Stout to reinforce the article's message. The sensual ad featured a bare-chested Hispanic man being stroked by a Hispanic woman whose lacy nightgown had fallen from her shoulder, exposing

much of her right breast. The man faced the camera directly, while the
woman's face was hidden by his head. This subservience plays on the
cultural dominance of Hispanic males.

According to Juana Mora, research analyst at the Los Angeles
County Office of Alcohol Programs, "In the case of alcohol advertising
to Latinos, there is a deliberate practice of influencing beliefs and
behaviors by appealing to 'cultural nostalgia'—traditions, images,
and norms that many of us grew up with."

In the same issue, a four-page article previewed a Latin American
art show that was about to begin a national tour. The tour sponsor
was Philip Morris, the nation's top tobacco company and number two
brewer. According to the article, Philip Morris supported the exhibi-
tion with a $350,000 grant, "as well as with marketing and public
relations assistance to reach out to the Hispanic community." Part of
that "marketing" included a full color, two-page ad in the center of the
magazine which prominently listed all the Philip Morris subsidiaries
sponsoring the tour.

Readers found yet another positive plug for Philip Morris on the
magazine's last page. In a full-page article titled "Our Mother Tongue,"
Frank Gomez, director of public affairs programs for Philip Morris,
decried the impact of Anglicisms on the Spanish language. "If indeed,
Spanish is so valuable, let us defend it, cherish it, nurture it, treat it as

*Many ads associate a product with
sexual success. In this Guinness
Stout ad, "dark, suggestive, and de-
licious" could refer either to the
models or the beer.*

we would our mother," Gomez concluded. "As we prepare to com-memorate the Quincentenary in 1992, we must protect our Spanish language, to use it as best we can and to encourage others to use it correctly." Not exactly controversial stuff, but a great piece of free public relations for Philip Morris.

Summing up health experts' concerns, Juana Mora said, "The problem with alcohol advertising is that it distorts the true impact of excessive and high-risk consumption on health. These powerful ad-vertising campaigns totally undermine the educational efforts of fami-lies, schools, and non-profit organizations."

Tobacco

As part of an extensive campaign to help Hispanics quit smoking, the Hispanic Smoking Cessation Research Project in San Francisco makes use of any free public-service advertising space it can arrange. But in early 1989, its ads were getting bumped off billboards and bus cards. Why? Because RJR Nabisco bought all the advertising space available to convince Mexican-Americans to smoke Newport ciga-rettes.

"Newport is everywhere," said Barbara Marin, director of the smoking cessation project. "We had a lot of trouble getting space because of the Newport campaign in the community."[23]

Public health officials from around the country say cigarette companies have undertaken a massive campaign to target Hispanics. The campaign has even included introduction in recent years of three cigarette brands with Spanish names that are reportedly aimed at Hispanics: Rio, Dorado, and L&M Superior.[24]

Those brands, along with big sellers in the Hispanic community such as Marlboro and Winston, are heavily advertised in Hispanic newspapers and magazines. "Hispanic magazines have an inordi-nately high density of cigarette advertisements, often stumping brands created especially for the community like Rio and Dorado," said Felipe Castro, associate professor at San Diego State University's Graduate School of Public Health.[25]

One of the major magazines for advertising by both tobacco and alcohol companies is *Vista,* a weekly newspaper supplement similar to *Parade* but written in English for Hispanics. In mid-1988, *Vista* had a circulation of 1.2 million and was carried in 27 newspapers.[26]

Industry experts say many Hispanic newspapers and magazines could not survive without cigarette and alcohol advertising. However, that economic dependence cannot help but affect the editorial content of the publications.

Al Marcus, associate director of the division of cancer control at UCLA's Jonsson Comprehensive Cancer Center, said it's bad enough that most Spanish-language magazines and newspapers accept advertising from tobacco companies. "But more importantly, they don't come out with criticisms of the tobacco industry, they don't come out with positions that advocate either abstinence or cessation."[27] Of course, mainstream publications such as *Time, Newsweek, Ms.,* and *The New Republic* are not any better.

In addition to advertising in Hispanic publications, tobacco companies also spend millions of dollars annually on billboards in Hispanic areas. "In the cities where we're intervening, cigarette advertising in Spanish is very prominent," said Dr. Emilio Carrillo, director of a smoking prevention project aimed primarily at Puerto Rican adolescents in Boston and Hartford, Conn.[28]

Carrillo, who is on the faculty of Harvard Medical School and the Harvard School of Public Health, said the heavy advertising is causing smoking rates to increase among Hispanic youths and women. "If you look at the billboard advertising in the Hispanic community, you will find that they all portray young, happy people who appear affluent, who appear very light-skinned," he said. "Basically, it's setting up billboards in poor, devastated communities showing pictures of wealth and well-being that are absolutely false in terms of what the billboards are advertising."

Dr. Harold Freeman, president of the American Cancer Society and chief of surgery at Harlem Hospital, said he's particularly troubled by where the billboards are placed. "Many times these billboards would be located in areas where children would naturally be," Freeman said. "We have photographs of billboards near schoolyards, and they're really showing youthful-looking people. Naturally, they're appealing to young people."[29]

Many experts say much of the tobacco advertising in Hispanic neighborhoods specifically targets youths. "I think it's a very vulnerable population," said Jane Garcia, of La Clinica de la Raza. "And it's being promoted as a very hip and cool thing to do."[30]

Some of the billboards show families in which the parents are smoking, said Castro, the professor at San Diego State University. The family image plays on the cultural belief in close-knit families, he said. "What better way to convince kids it's OK to smoke than to have uncle or parent figures participating along with the kids as smokers?" he said.[31]

Billboards like these are partly responsible for rising smoking and cancer rates among Hispanics.

Marin said all the billboards she sees in Hispanic neighborhoods seem to be targeting youths. "I have trouble imagining that any of them aren't directed at Hispanic youth because they're all done with models who are in their early 20s," she said. "And who else are youth going to be looking for? They're not looking for kids necessarily their own age who might still be pimply."

The tobacco companies have no choice but to target children, according to Kenneth Warner, a professor in the University of Michigan's School of Public Health and author of the book *Selling Smoke:*

Cigarette Advertising and Public Health. Warner also served as senior scientific editor for *Reducing the Health Consequences of Smoking: 25 Years of Progress,* a report released in January 1989 by U.S. Surgeon General C. Everett Koop.

Warner said he suspects that more than 90 percent of smokers start smoking as pre-teens or teenagers. "We're talking about an industry that lives or dies on the number of new smokers, and the new smoking population comes almost exclusively from kids," he said. "While that doesn't say that advertising targets children, it certainly suggests that there's a powerful incentive to target children because if you don't get children smoking, you don't have smokers."[32]

The tobacco industry vehemently denies assertions by public health officials that billboards in Hispanic neighborhoods specifically target youths. "They have the general allegation that cigarette advertising is geared toward youth," said Gary Miller, the Tobacco Institute spokesman. "Then they try to fragment it and say Hispanic advertising is geared toward Hispanic youth, Black advertising is geared toward Black youth. In general, they keep claiming youth, youth, youth. And again, that wasn't found to be the case."

Youthful-looking models in magazine ads promote smoking among boys and girls. The rates of cancer related to smoking are increasing rapidly among Hispanics.

Miller said hearings before Congress in the summer of 1987 on a bill to restrict tobacco advertising proved that such factors as peer pressure and parental influence — not advertising — cause kids to smoke. "If there's any effect advertising has, it's *de minimis*," Miller said.[33]

The cigarette companies aren't just going after Hispanic children, however. "It's our impression that Hispanics, especially Hispanic females, are really being targeted," said Neill Piland, who directs a smoking-intervention program in Santa Fe, New Mexico. Cigarette advertising now features many more young Hispanic women than it did before, he said. Why are the cigarette companies specifically targeting Hispanic women? Piland thinks it's because Hispanic women have traditionally smoked less than their White and Black counterparts.[34]

So what impact does all this targeting have? Freeman, the American Cancer Society president, said the targeting causes people to take up smoking. "The increase in smoking rates in women in general in America, not looking at race or culture, occurred just after the women were made targets by advertisers," he said. "So I think there's a strong suggestion that smoking by American women of all cultures increased at the same time that the advertising began to target women."[35]

In *Reducing the Health Consequences of Smoking: 25 Years of Progress*, Surgeon General Koop said there is "no scientifically rigorous study available to the public that provides a definitive answer to the basic question of whether advertising and promotion increase the level of tobacco consumption." The difficulties inherent in conducting such a study mean "none is likely to be forthcoming in the foreseeable future," the report said.

However, Koop still determined that cigarette advertising probably causes increased consumption. "The most comprehensive review of both the direct and indirect mechanisms concluded that the collective empirical, experiential and logical evidence makes it more likely than not that advertising and promotional activities do stimulate consumption," the report said. "However, that analysis also concluded that the extent of influence of advertising and promotion on the level of consumption is unknown and possibly unknowable."[36]

Miller, of the Tobacco Institute, said Koop's report supports the Institute's position that no scientific study proves there's a connection between advertising and cigarette consumption. When asked about Koop's statement that evidence shows there probably is a link, Miller said: "Now, I don't know if there's something else he said also in the report that says there's other evidence that says a link, but he just said there's no scientifically rigorous study available to the public that provides a definitive answer to the basic question of whether advertising or promotion increases the level of tobacco consumption."

Attempts by Miller and others to distort the Surgeon General's findings annoy Kenneth Warner, who served as senior scientific editor for the report. "The Surgeon General's report says that there is essentially no 'smoking gun' that proves definitively one way or another how much consumption is influenced by advertising," Warner said. "But it does say that the most thorough review of the evidence, and looking at the evidence in its entirety, suggests there is an association."[37]

The tobacco industry also likes to say that public health authorities and others who express concerns about smoking rates in minority groups are showing a lack of respect for minorities. "I think it's absolutely paternalistic for someone to say that tobacco advertising and tobacco support affects Blacks, Hispanics, or women different than they do White men," said Brennan Moran, a spokesperson for the Tobacco Institute.[38]

Freeman, who is himself Black, said the tobacco industry has things turned around. "There's nothing more paternalistic than a corporate power selling a lethal product coming into a community and indicating that somebody should smoke," Freeman said. "The 'Great White Father' coming into a community of a certain culture and saying in various images that in order to be successful, in order to be happy and sophisticated this is what you should do, that's paternalism."[39]

Junk Foods

Most soft drink and fast food companies started targeting Hispanics long after the alcohol and tobacco industries zeroed in on the market, but they're now trying to make up for lost time.

PepsiCo made history during the 1989 Grammy Awards when it ran the first Spanish-language ad on mainstream television. The ad featured Puerto Rican teen idol Chayanne. Pepsi has also used such superstars as Michael Jackson, Tina Turner, and the group Menudo in Spanish-language television ads run on the two Spanish networks in the United States and in Latin America.[40]

Pepsi also ran a tremendously successful advertising promotion

Procter & Gamble products are featured throughout Cocina Crisco *(Crisco Kitchen). High-fat, high-calorie foods and recipes contribute to obesity and diabetes.*

on Univision, the Spanish-language television network. The promotion involved a contest where viewers sent in letters to be placed in a drawing for $150,000 toward a "dream house." For 11 weeks before the drawing, Pepsi ran nine TV spots weekly to promote the contest, generating more than 250,000 entries. "The effect on sales can't be measured yet, but we generated a phenomenal number of entries," said the promotions manager for the Hispanic advertising agency that

Soft-drink companies are tapping into the Hispanic market in a big way. Pepsi and Coke contain ten teaspoons of sugar per can.

designed the contest. "We started with a normal-size raffle drum and had to transfer to a swimming pool."[41]

Ironically, both Pepsi and Coca-Cola sponsor school dropout prevention programs with celebrity figureheads and nearly identical names. Pepsi's program is called simply the "Stay In School Program," while Coke's is called the "Coca-Cola Fernando Valenzuela 'Be Smart, Stay-In-School' Program." Both Pepsi and Coke have run full-page ads in Hispanic magazines touting the programs and, incidentally, the companies that sponsor them.

Coke's ads feature Fernando Valenzuela, the Mexican-American pitching star for the Los Angeles Dodgers. "We are proud to have Fernando on our team," the Coke ad says. "And determined to help other Hispanics reach their goals. Together, we're helping make America stronger."[42]

The Pepsi ad features Edward James Olmos, star of the "Miami Vice" TV show. The ad, after urging adults to help children decide to stay in school, closes with the line: "Make the choice of the new generation: Education." The line is a take-off on Pepsi's slogan: "The choice of a new generation."[43]

PepsiCo also has run a full-page corporate image ad promoting the "BOOK IT!" national reading incentive program, which is sponsored by its Pizza Hut division. The ad shows six Hispanic youngsters eating in a Pizza Hut restaurant. Headlined "PepsiCo: Serving the New Generation," the ad also features logos for five PepsiCo divisions: Pepsi, Frito-Lay, Pizza Hut, Taco Bell, and Kentucky Fried Chicken.[44]

In the fast-food industry, McDonald's was the first franchise to target Hispanics. The company, which began advertising in Spanish in 1976, was committed to the Hispanic market "long before it became a fad," a McDonald's spokesman noted.[45] The early involvement has resulted in McDonald's dominating the other burger chains in the Hispanic market segment,[46] as it also does in the general market.

Most recently, McDonald's signed an economic agreement with the Hispanic Association on Corporate Responsibility (HACER), a coalition of seven national Hispanic organizations. Under the agreement, McDonald's pledged to increase the percentage of Hispanics in its work force to nine percent, up from less than six percent when the pact was signed in late 1988. McDonald's also agreed to increase its procurement from Hispanic suppliers and to expand its business with Hispanic-owned banks, marketing and public relations agencies, and construction companies. More franchises also will be made available to Hispanics. Some 130 restaurants were managed by Hispanics in

1988, and the goal is to open 90 Hispanic-run restaurants in 1989. The pact is supposed to represent at least $200 million in benefits to Hispanics over five years.[47]

Hispanic groups signing the agreement included the Cuban American National Council, American G.I. Forum, National IMAGE, National Puerto Rican Coalition, League of United Latin American Citizens (LULAC), National Association of Hispanic Publications, and National Council of La Raza.

McDonald's also has been at the forefront of creating special advertisements directed at Hispanics. Bicultural advertising "reached a new level of sophistication," according to *Hispanic Business*, with an English-language McDonald's television spot that appealed to Whites while also containing a special message for Hispanics. The ad, titled "Claudia's Birthday," appeared to the general audience to simply show a Hispanic girl celebrating her birthday. To Hispanics, though, it was apparent the girl was celebrating her 15th birthday, a symbolic "coming of age" known as a *quinceanera*.[48]

Corporate image ads that McDonald's runs in Hispanic publications tout the company's involvement in the Hispanic community. "By accepting us into the Hispanic community and making McDonald's part of your life, you've helped us to grow and prosper," says one ad. "We believe in sharing our success by giving something back to the community we serve." The ad lists programs supported by McDonald's such as the "Musical Heritage of Latin America" school program; Hispanic Heritage Week, when McDonald's commissions a Hispanic

McDonald's is a heavy advertiser on Spanish-language television. These ads tout (l) the high-calorie McChicken sandwich and (r) salads, the latter being one of the few commercials for a healthful food.

artist to create a theme poster for its restaurants; and the Ronald McDonald House.[49]

McDonald's involvement in the community may pay off handsomely for the company in coming years, according to Jerry Apodaca, president of HACER, the group that negotiated the economic agreement with McDonald's. "They may be facing the problems of cholesterol in the next ten years, and campaigns not to eat french fries," he said. "If that ever happens, they'll be way ahead of the game because they're very active in the community."[50]

Taking a cue from McDonald's success, Domino's Pizza announced in 1987 that it was undertaking a major marketing effort to attract Hispanic consumers. The $2 million budgeted for the campaign was double the amount the entire pizza industry spent to attract Hispanics in the previous year.[51] The Domino's campaign included Spanish-language advertising on television, radio, and newspapers, in addition to direct mail, door hangers, and flyers.[52]

In the March 1989 issue of *Hispanic* magazine, Domino's used a full-page ad to announce a national essay contest for high-school students on the theme, "What it means to be Hispanic." The grand prize winner will receive a $2,000 college scholarship, a trip for four to Washington, D.C. for the awards presentation, and free pizza for a year.[53]

Other fast-food chains also are starting to target the Hispanic market. Some of the other chains with advertising programs aimed at Hispanics include Burger King, Wendy's, Kentucky Fried Chicken, and Pizza Hut.[54] Candy companies, whose products also tend to be loaded with fat and sugar, also are getting their message out to Hispanics. Ads for Snickers, Hershey's Kisses, M&Ms, and other candies fill TV screens, as do ads for such "breakfast candies" as Honey-Comb, Lucky Charms, and Cocoa Puffs.

But simply advertising on television or in a magazine isn't enough anymore for the disease-promoting companies. As they try to increase their ties to the Hispanic community, many companies are turning to event marketing, as we shall see in the next chapter.

4

Event Marketing

The Puerto Rican Festival is the largest cultural and social event of the year for Boston's Hispanic community. To Dr. Emilio Carrillo, it looked like a great opportunity to educate Hispanic youths about the hazards of smoking.

Carrillo, a faculty member at Harvard Medical School and the Harvard School of Public Health, directs a smoking prevention program aimed primarily at Puerto Rican adolescents in Boston and Hartford. The program is funded by the National Cancer Institute.

Carrillo told the festival organizers his program would like to set up a booth with educational materials. "We found resistance from the organizers of the festival," Carrillo said. Why was that? "They felt that letting us participate would risk their losing sponsorship by the tobacco company."[1]

Tobacco or alcohol companies always sponsored the festival. "Tobacco companies have over the years competed with each other to sponsor this event," he said. Carrillo believes tobacco companies paid $30,000 or more to be named the festival sponsor.

After weeks of political struggle that involved calls to the mayor's office and community agencies, Carrillo was told his program was still banned from the festival, because a tobacco company wouldn't sponsor the event if his booth was allowed. But there was good news, too: The tobacco company would not be sponsoring the festival.

Carrillo still doesn't know whether the tobacco company pulled out on its own or if the festival organizers threw out the cigarette company because they suddenly felt a pang of conscience over having their event sponsored by a disease-promoting company. Whatever the reason, Carrillo chalks up the outcome as a victory. "A lot of feathers were ruffled and a lot of phone calls were made and the sponsorship did not happen," he said. "We were slapped on the wrist by not being able to be present, but they were not present either."

Other health professionals attempting to conduct smoking intervention efforts at Hispanic festivals also have come face-to-face with the tobacco companies. "When we go to any kind of festival, we're always elbowing the people giving out free cigarettes," said Barbara Marin, director of the Hispanic Smoking Cessation Research Project in San Francisco. "I don't think we've ever been to a community thing that didn't have massive amounts of freebies from the tobacco industry. And the major celebrations are partially sponsored by the tobacco industry, so they actually get in up front."[2]

At the last festival she attended in San Francisco, Marin said, tobacco company representatives were throwing free cigarette samples into the crowd. "Everybody was just grabbing them," she said. "They didn't care if they were 21, whether they were smokers or not, they were just giving them to everybody."

Today, it sometimes seems that the gathering of two or more Hispanics in one spot is enough incentive to get the alcohol and tobacco companies to roll in event booths and start handing out free cigarettes and beer. Promotional activities now play a major role in efforts to hook Hispanics, and in the last few years alcohol and tobacco companies have sponsored everything from community festivals and concerts to Hispanic art tours and domino tournaments. Soft-drink companies are also becoming active in event sponsorship.

Some of the events have been virtually created by alcohol or tobacco companies as marketing tools. For example, the Mexican holiday Cinco de Mayo, which commemorates the defeat of French invaders by a Mexican force on May 5, 1862, is hardly noticed in Mexico. But that didn't stop United States companies from using the holiday as the excuse for a marketing extravaganza.

"Until 10 years ago, Cinco de Mayo was largely ignored by the non-Latin community," said an article in *USA Today*. "Then, perhaps because there were few other spring marketing opportunities or because they just realized what an untapped market Hispanics were, several large beer and soft-drink companies began sponsoring local events. Others soon joined them, eventually turning Cinco de Mayo into a Mexican St. Patrick's Day."

In 1988, companies spent $25 million on promotions during the holiday in southern California alone. Some of the biggest spenders: PepsiCo, Coca-Cola, Adolph Coors, Anheuser-Busch, and Stroh Brewery.[3]

LA Times 5/8/89

AREA

Cinco de Mayo cut short when crowds get rowdy

The third day of Cinco de Mayo festivities downtown and in Lincoln Park was canceled early last night due to drunkenness and violence, including a shooting and rock and bottle throwing in which at least six people were injured, police said.

Thousands of visitors had gathered about 4 p.m. for a concert and festival at Lincoln Park when drunken gang members began throwing rocks and bottles in front of the stage, Sgt. George Spitzer said.

A few minutes later shots were fired near the crowd from a car driving down Valley Boulevard in front of the park, Spitzer said.

At 9 p.m. the downtown Cinco de Mayo festivities along Olvera Street also were cut short by an hour due to public drunkenness, Sgt. Jim Leinen said.

BELVEDERE PARK
SATURDAY MAY 6 11 AM to 8 PM
SUNDAY MAY 7 11 AM to 8 PM

CINCO de MAYO CELEBRATION
MUSIC ★ FOOD ★ FUN

OLVERA STREET
FRIDAY MAY 5 12 PM TO 10 PM
SATURDAY MAY 6 11 AM to 10 PM
SUNDAY MAY 7 11 AM to 10 PM

(l) Before 1989 Cinco de Mayo festivities in Los Angeles, ads for Budweiser (and Miller) beer encouraged attendance and drinking. (r) The next day, newspaper articles described the predictable drunken brawls that occurred.

In 1989 Anheuser-Busch and Miller sponsored Cinco de Mayo festivities in Los Angeles that turned into drunken brawls. The Miller-sponsored concert in Lincoln Park was cut short by rock and bottle throwing and a shooting that injured at least six people and led to one shooting death later in the evening. Ray Chavira, a Los Angeles County probation officer and anti-drug activist, told the *Los Angeles Times* that Cinco de Mayo is "a Mickey Mouse holiday ... What about the real reason for celebrating it? They're pushing a legalized drug [beer] upon our community. You're asking for trouble."[4]

The emphasis on drinking during Cinco de Mayo has been criticized by some Hispanic leaders. In a column in the *Los Angeles Herald Examiner*, Rodolfo Acuna, professor of Chicano studies at California State University-Northridge, wrote: "This month, both barrio and yuppie bars advertised Cinco de Mayo 'Happy Hours,' and margaritas and beer flowed freely. In good old American fashion, the celebration has been packaged and marketed to the public." Alcohol also was the primary focus of a concert featuring Hispanic groups held the weekend before the Cinco de Mayo festivities began. "Occasionally, there was the faint cry of 'Viva el Cinco de Mayo' and 'Viva la Raza!'" Acuna wrote. "More often, it was Miller time."[5]

Specialized publications of the marketing industry make it clear that the major focus of many of the promotions undertaken by beer and tobacco companies is on getting free samples into the hands of potential customers. "Coors sponsors a multitude of special events that offer consumers a unique opportunity to sample its product," says the book *Successful Marketing to U.S. Hispanics and Asians*, published by the American Management Association. The book quotes Frank Solis, then head of Coors' community relations department, as saying: "There are a lot of people out there who, prior to these special events, have never sampled our product."[6]

Both Philip Morris and Stroh look to events for their sampling possibilities, according to an article in *Sales and Marketing Management* magazine. In the story, a Philip Morris spokesperson is quoted as saying the company has a list of requirements for sponsoring an event. The event has to be national in scope, consistent with a brand image, a popular spectator activity, and must offer sampling possibilities, according to the article. "We also weigh the news value of an event," the spokesperson said. "Will the papers and magazines write stories about it?" The article also quotes the vice president of marketing services for Stroh Brewery as saying: "When we evaluate possible event sponsorship, the questions we ask are, 'Is it our target audience? Is it repeatable? Does it provide sampling opportunities?' And certainly not least important, 'Is it media-driven?' "[7]

Other motives for sponsoring events are thinly veiled in industry trade journals. An article in *Tobacco Reporter* about Winston cigarettes, made by RJR Nabisco, notes that it sponsors numerous Hispanic festivals across the country. Winston's sponsorship involves financial contributions to the sponsoring groups, according to the magazine, "and it also means a direct involvement in Hispanic community and business affairs." The senior brand manager for Winston is quoted as saying: "Our efforts reflect a growing practice of local groups and private enterprises joining hands to preserve a heritage and, at the same time, improve life in the communities in which Hispanics live."[8]

TV commercials for cigarettes are illegal, but tobacco companies know how to evade the regulations. Race cars, too, are emblazoned with the names of cigarette brands.

Event marketing and promotions are particularly important to the tobacco industry, which is banned by law from advertising on television, and the liquor industry, which voluntarily abstains from broadcast advertising. Promotional expenditures by the tobacco companies doubled between 1980 and 1983, and by 1986 they spent about $1 billion on promotions directed at various audiences.[9] In1985 alone, RJR Nabisco sponsored more than 1,600 events in 200 cities aimed at a wide assortment of groups.[10]

Examples of some of the promotions undertaken by tobacco companies to woo Hispanic consumers show the diversity of their efforts:

- When Liggett & Myers Tobacco Co. introduced Dorado, a cigarette aimed at Hispanics, it hired a New Mexico marketing consultant whose connnections helped get Dorado promotions into the state fair, a hot-air balloon festival, and the annual Santa Fe fiesta.[11]

- Marlboro has sponsored a series of charreadas, or Mexican rodeos, at state fairs throughout California. The program is said to have given the brand a "high profile" at "minimal expense" — about $250,000.[12] The brand also sponsors the Marlboro Soccer Cup, which involves the world's top soccer teams.[13]

- Philip Morris, which markets Marlboro, Virginia Slims, Benson & Hedges, Merit, Parliament Lights, and other brands, annually publishes *A Guide to Hispanic Organizations*. The guide, which is filled with ads for Philip Morris' cigarettes, lists Hispanic civic, business, professional and educational groups.

- Philip Morris is sponsoring a national art tour called "The Latin American Spirit: Art and Artists in the United States, 1920–1970." Philip Morris provided a $350,000 grant for the tour, which will travel to museums in New York, Texas, California, Florida, and Puerto Rico.[14]

All the promotional activities help cigarette companies create an image that is inaccurate, according to Kenneth Warner, professor at the University of Michigan's School of Public Health. In his book, *Selling Smoke: Cigarette Advertising and Public Health*, Warner wrote: "Perhaps the least well-defined but potentially most important institutional impact of cigarette companies' promotions is their contribution to creating an aura of legitimacy, of wholesomeness, for an industry that produces a product that annually accounts for about a fifth of all American deaths."[15]

The alcohol industry is at least equally aggressive in using event marketing and promotions to push its products. Some of these activities include:

- Coors is sponsoring "The 1989 Coors National Hispanic Art Exhibit and Tour," which will visit museums in California, New Mexico, and Florida.[16]

- Coors also sponsors about four dances each year in Miami, each of which draws thousands of people. It also co-sponsored the city's Hispanic Heritage paella festival, where it served 15,400 glasses of beer.[17] In 1988, the company expected to spend $180,000 on events in Miami alone.[18]

- Miller Lite has sponsored the Puerto Rican Day parade and the Puerto Rican handicapped children's telethon, both in New York; salsa concerts in New York, Chicago, San Francisco, Los

Hispanic parades, such as this one in New York City, usually feature floats sponsored by liquor companies.

Angeles, and Miami; and Mexican concerts and boxing championships in Texas and California.[19]

- Anheuser-Busch, which produces such beers as Budweiser, Bud Light and Michelob, has sponsored an entire stage for musical acts at Miami's Calle Ocho festival.

- Hiram Walker Inc., distiller of Canadian Club whisky, sponsored "The Canadian Club Hispanic Art Tour," which reached New York, Texas, and California.[20]

- In New York City, Somerset Importers Ltd., importer of Johnnie Walker scotch, Tanqueray gin, and Appleton rum, sponsors domino tournaments, amateur baseball leagues, and a soccer league. The company also participates in festivals and parades. "Whatever the parade — Cuban, Dominican or Puerto Rican — Somerset's Johnnie Walker is there," said an article in *Liquor Store* magazine.[21]

The alcohol and tobacco companies spend millions of dollars annually on promotional activities aimed at Hispanics. Equally important, but far less expensive, are the contributions they give to major national Hispanic organizations, as the next chapter explains.

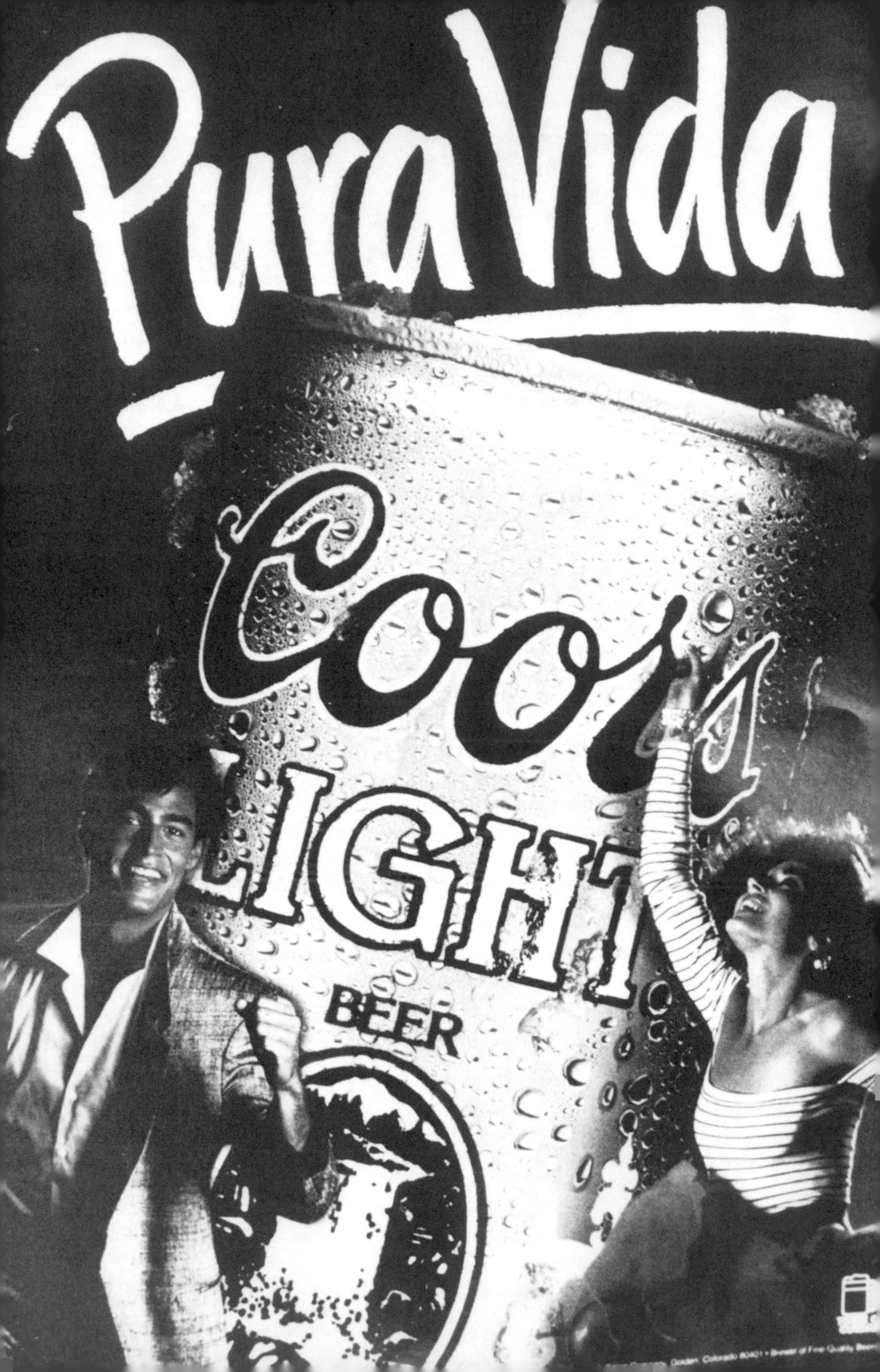
Pura Vida
BEER

5

Contributions To Hispanic Organizations

C onservatively estimated, alcohol, tobacco, fast-food, and soft-drink companies annually give well over $1 million to Hispanic organizations in direct contributions and conference sponsorships. The figure is most likely a great deal higher, and could be as much as several million dollars.

The bulk of the money comes from alcohol and tobacco companies, which have long been at the forefront of corporate giving to Hispanic and Black groups. However, fast-food and soft-drink companies are becoming increasingly important as corporate donors.

The companies say they give the money simply because they want to be good corporate citizens and to support worthy causes. Leaders of Hispanic organizations say they need the money for two reasons: most corporate donors still ignore the Hispanic community, and budget cuts by the Reagan administration slashed grants and contracts that many Hispanic groups relied upon.

However, public health officials and other critics, many of them within the Hispanic community, say the contributions have effectively silenced national organizations on critical health issues facing Hispanics. They express particular concern about contributions from alcohol and tobacco companies in light of the severe alcohol problems in the community and the increase in cancer rates.

Although alcohol and tobacco companies have been contributing to Hispanic organizations for years, few people have questioned the propriety of soliciting or accepting the money. "It's a question no one has raised in our community, and no one has come to terms with or discussed," said Arnoldo Torres, national political director of the League of United Latin American Citizens (LULAC), the nation's oldest and largest Hispanic organization. Torres was LULAC's executive director from 1979 to 1985.[1]

Questions haven't been raised about alcohol and tobacco money at least in part because other types of corporations have largely ignored Hispanic groups, said Marilyn Aguirre-Molina, an assistant professor at the University of Medicine and Dentistry of New Jersey who has directed an alcohol prevention program for Hispanic adolescents. "Nobody is out there," she said. "So when you have somebody who's willing to give you money and you need that money to operate, you're not going to scrutinize that much." But lately, she said, "I've been getting more and more people saying, 'Hey, we're in a bind. Can you get us some money other than from alcohol and tobacco companies?'"[2]

William Diaz, a program officer for the Ford Foundation who has been involved in Hispanic grantmaking for six years, said philanthropists have only become interested in Hispanics in recent years. "When corporations and foundations have thought about minority, they've thought about Black," he said. "It's only been since 1980 that Hispanics have really been on the philanthropic consciousness."[3]

Many Hispanic organizations relied heavily on government contracts and grants until the Reagan administration started cutting the federal budget, said Raul Yzaguirre, president of the National Council of La Raza, one of the largest and most prominent Hispanic groups. "When the federal cuts came in '81 and '82, Hispanic organizations were devastated, disproportionately hurt," he said. "Quite a few simply ceased to exist."[4]

But while the federal government was cutting spending and most corporations were ignoring Hispanics, the alcohol and tobacco companies were always there to help out with a contribution. Their heavy involvement in the Hispanic community continues today. "They're out there pitching, there's no doubt about it," said Michael Cortes, a founder of Hispanics in Philanthropy and former vice president of the National Council of La Raza.[5]

Today, however, the serious health problems in the Hispanic community are leading some Hispanic activists and public health officials to start questioning the propriety of accepting money from alcohol and tobacco companies. Torres, of LULAC, said he finds "unsettling" the acceptance of money from those companies. "We give them a tremendous amount of visibility, almost an endorsement at times, because the functions we hold are so public and they sponsor the big functions," he said. "It is somewhat of a worry to know that the products they are pushing are products that really are not in our best interest."[6]

In testimony before a congressional subcommittee, Jane Delgado, executive director of the National Coalition of Hispanic Health and Human Services Organizations (COSSMHO), decried the influence of tobacco money. "...[O]ften the foundations set up by these companies have been there where no one else has been," she said. "This makes it very hard for people to speak out against tobacco and its many uses."[7] Financial support from other corporations and foundations is meager, Delgado said, leaving the door open for the tobacco industry. "...[T]he dismal record of financial support for Hispanic organizations and institutions has created a situation of vulnerability," Delgado told the subcommittee. "It is very difficult for any of our groups to refuse contributions from the tobacco industry when so few options are available."[8]

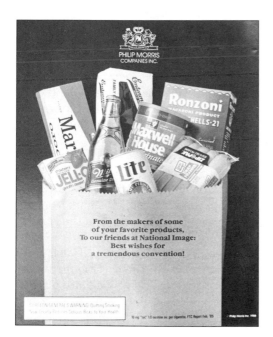

Philip Morris, Anheuser-Busch, Stroh, Coors, PepsiCo, and other companies support Hispanic organizations through sponsorship of image-ads like this one in magazines and convention programs.

Many health experts working in the Hispanic community oppose the contributions. "It's a sad state of affairs that minority organizations and agencies have to turn to purveyors of death for support, support that they cannot find elsewhere," said Dr. Emilio Carrillo, a faculty member at Harvard Medical School and the Harvard School of Public Health. All Hispanics are concerned about the tragic impact AIDS is having on the Hispanic community, he said, yet few know or care that smoking-related ailments such as cardiovascular disease, cancer, and strokes are killing far more Hispanics than AIDS.[9]

Dr. Al Marcus, of UCLA's Jonsson Comprehensive Cancer Center, said the tobacco companies aren't just seeking to gain goodwill with their contributions. "I think it's a blatant attempt to buy influence," he said. "I think it is working."[10]

Dr. Harold Freeman, president of the American Cancer Society and a leading Black physician, is well aware of tobacco industry support for minority groups. "I think it's a very sensitive issue," Freeman said. "We believe that even if they are forced at least for the time being to accept this money, that they are still obligated to educate their constituents on any matter that has a deep effect on the quality of life and survival of those people."[11]

Dr. Raul Caetano, senior scientist at the Alcohol Research Group in San Francisco, said corporate contributions discourage Hispanic organizations from getting involved in alcohol abuse prevention. "I would prefer that they did not get any money from the alcohol industry," he said. "I think if that was the case, then they would probably be more free to speak out against exaggeration and targeting of Hispanics by the alcohol advertising. As it is, because they're getting that money, they can't say anything about it. And if they don't say anything, then one begins to suspect that they don't say anything because they're getting the money."[12]

Leaders of national Hispanic organizations deny that the contributions buy silence. "I don't know of any organization that has been unduly influenced by sources of money," said Yzaguirre, La Raza's president. About $100,000 of his group's $3 million annual budget comes from alcohol and tobacco companies, he said, and the companies also sponsor dances, luncheons, and other events at La Raza's annual convention. La Raza also administers an annual $50,000 grant from RJR Nabisco that goes directly to affiliates, Yzaguirre said, although "some of our local affiliates that are very much into alcohol abuse prevention and health have indicated they don't want to receive any money that comes directly or indirectly from alcohol or tobacco.

"Our posture is we're not going to be influenced by any company, or by any government agency," Yzaguirre added. "We just make it very clear that our public policy postures are going to be driven by the facts and nothing else. And we're fortunate that our funding base is so diversified that we're not worried about undue pressure from any one source." Currently, La Raza has no program aimed at alcohol and tobacco.[13]

Some leaders of Hispanic groups complain that the issue of receiving support from alcohol and tobacco companies is blown out of proportion. "If you were to call something 'dirty money,' I would be much more concerned about companies that pollute the environment," said Frank Newton, president of the National Association of Hispanic Journalists.[14] Newton said his group gets about $25,000 a year in general support from alcohol and tobacco companies, in addition to money for its annual conference.

For several years, the association received an annual grant of $10,000 from Philip Morris, Newton said. In an interview with *Los Angeles Times* reporter Myron Levin, Newton said: "Philip Morris gave us money and hasn't asked for any special consideration. I'm less concerned about taking money from Philip Morris. . . than the fact that a lot of these big media companies don't give a dime."[15] Philip Morris no longer awards the grant, Newton said.

One group that doesn't solicit money from alcohol and tobacco companies is the Hispanic Policy Development Project, a Washington, D.C.-based organization that focuses on education and employment issues. "It's not a policy of the board or anything like that," said Rafael Valdivieso, vice president for program and research. "But we've always stayed away from that kind of money."[16] The Interamerican College of Physicians and Surgeons and the UCLA Chicano Studies Research Center are two other groups that do not receive alcohol and tobacco funding.

The National Association for Chicano Studies specifically rejected alcohol and tobacco industry funding for its 1989 conference, despite vigorous lobbying by several brewers.[17] The association's site committee recognized that alcohol is a major killer that also impedes intellectual development.

Louis Nunez, president of the National Puerto Rican Coalition, said alcohol and tobacco companies expect something in return for their donations. "It's not a quid pro quo situation, you don't sign anything," he said. "It's sort of understood that you're going to work with them. . . Obviously, the tobacco industry is very involved in

Billboards are unavoidable — you can't just flip the page or turn off a switch to make the ads disappear.

legislation, and I would assume that any organization that takes a very strong position against the use of tobacco, not even a strong position but a public position, would not get their support."[18] The coalition recently received a three-year, $75,000 grant from Philip Morris that will be used to hire a young college graduate each year to work as a Capitol Hill lobbyist.[19]

Companies that make contributions are now much more worried about the bottom line than they used to be, according to Newton. "It used to be here's some money, do something that's worthwhile, and we would like some visibility and people will think we're a nice company and that kind of stuff," Newton said. "Now, it's how many cans of beer am I going to be able to sell if I give you money? What can you show me that's going to increase the sale of my product if I support this activity that you asked for?"[20]

Jerry Apodaca, who heads the Hispanic Association on Corporate Responsibility (HACER), said alcohol and tobacco companies also make contributions because "they need friends." He explained that "When they give this money, part of it is genuine corporate responsibility and some social commitment. They've got to be looking for some return, and I don't think there's anything wrong with that. In spite of the dilemmas of the tobacco companies or the beer companies or the scotch companies or the bourbon companies, they are not illegal." Apodaca's sympathetic words are not surprising, considering that he served on Philip Morris' board of directors from 1979 to 1982.[21]

Tony Bonilla, a former president of LULAC, said it would be wrong for Hispanic organizations to reject money from certain types of corporations. "I think the Hispanic community cannot afford to just turn their back on these companies who have been our friends over the years by saying well, now that we know that the product you sell can be injurious to our health, we don't want your help," he said. "I think a more responsible approach to use is we recognize that excessive use of your product can be injurious to our health, and we want you to help us spread the word. And I think the companies will do it."

Yet close ties to the tobacco and alcohol industries have sometimes caused problems for Hispanic organizations. In 1985, Joseph Trevino, then executive director of LULAC, appeared on a videotape prepared by the Tobacco Institute designed to persuade members of Congress not to raise excise taxes on cigarettes. In his presentation, Trevino said excise taxes had a disproportionate impact on the poor. At no point was there any mention on the tape that it was sponsored by the Tobacco Institute.[22]

A year later, LULAC leaders approved a resolution opposing workplace smoking rules that "restrict the personal freedoms of Hispanic employees in the workplace," according to an article by Myron Levin of the *Los Angeles Times.* The Tobacco Institute instructed members of its field staff to use the resolution to rally "LULAC chapters and ... Hispanic Chambers of Commerce in states and localities considering workplace smoking restrictions." Both LULAC and the Hispanic Chambers have received contributions from the tobacco industry.[23]

Trevino's appearance on the videotape and passage of the workplace smoking resolution anger LULAC's Torres. "He presented himself to do the commercial with the Tobacco Institute," Torres said. "There's no doubt what he was doing. He was basically angling for a good job in the private sector." That's exactly what he got. Today, Trevino is an account supervisor for the marketing giant Fleischman-Hillard Inc. in St. Louis. When people call Anheuser-Busch to learn about the firm's Hispanic marketing program, they are transferred to Trevino at Fleischman-Hillard. Trevino services other accounts as well, including — not surprisingly — some tobacco accounts.

Torres said the workplace smoking resolution was not initiated by LULAC, but by industry. He added that the videotape and resolution hurt LULAC. "There's no integrity in that; I think any human being would recognize that. You would never see something like that happening in this organization today," he said.

Trevino defended his actions in an interview with the *National Journal*. "If someone chooses to view it as prostitution, then Washington is full of prostitutes," he said. "I'm not uncomfortable, embarrassed, or guilty about anything. . . If you live and work in Washington, D.C., you reach out for coalitions—you don't live and work by yourself."[24]

The Tobacco Institute says the concern over workplace smoking rules originated with LULAC, and denies that it used LULAC as a front group. "That's just another allegation used to help buttress the efforts of anti-smokers," said Gary Miller, assistant to the president. "They'll hit anything they can, as absurd as it can be sometimes." According to some observers, the tobacco industry's real motivation in seeking LULAC's help in fighting workplace smoking rules was to turn a health issue into a civil rights issue.

Alcohol and tobacco companies also are using their money to meddle in the internal politics of Hispanic groups, according to Jose Antonio Font, president emeritus of the Ibero-American Chamber of Commerce in Washington, D.C. That organization, a local group, in 1987 accused the U.S. Hispanic Chamber of Commerce of encroaching on local chamber activities. When its protest failed to result in changes, the Ibero-American chamber threatened to form a rival National Confederation of Hispanic-American Chambers of Commerce. At about the same time, the Ibero-American chamber applied for a grant from Philip Morris to fund a program to teach refugee children from El Salvador what it meant to be an American.

"The message came back: If you mess around with the U.S. Hispanic Chamber, forget about any kind of relationship," said Font, who was a founder of the U.S. Hispanic Chamber and served as its first vice president. Philip Morris wanted to protect the U.S. Hispanic Chamber, Font said, because the group gives the company good publicity in the Hispanic community.[25]

Indeed it does. A cover picture on the September 1987 issue of *Hispanic Business,* an independent magazine, showed the chamber president with two top officials of Philip Morris and an executive of Miller Brewing, a Philip Morris subsidiary.[26] Three months later, the magazine ran another picture of the four men "meeting in New York to plan the 8th Annual Convention of the U.S. Hispanic Chamber of Commerce." In the picture, one of the men is holding a beer bottle, another holds a beer can, and two more bottles and a cigarette package containing Philip Morris products are prominently featured on the conference table where the men are gathered.[27]

At the 1988 convention of the U.S. Hispanic Chamber of Commerce, Miller Brewing presented the chamber with a $100,000 donation, and Miller joined with its parent, Philip Morris, in sponsoring the closing banquet. In return, the chamber named Miller's manager of Hispanic marketing its "Corporate Hispanic Advocate of the Year."[28]

Conventions are made into huge marketing events by alcohol, tobacco, fast-food, and soft-drink companies, which rent booths, buy ads in the convention programs, and sponsor lunches, dinners and dances. Many of the beer companies have booths that look like bars and dispense free beer both day and night. "They all do it," said Nunez, of the National Puerto Rican Coalition. "It's a very major kind of expense for the beer companies."

Jose Cuellar, study director of the United States-Mexican Families and Alcohol Project at the Prevention Research Center in California, learned about the influence of alcohol companies in 1988 when he attended the annual conference of the National Council of La Raza. One of the luncheons was sponsored by Budweiser. "They not only promoted it in terms of little flyers with notices that we're sponsoring the event, but there were actually buckets of ice with cans of Bud Light on every table for the noon luncheon," Cuellar said. "It was certainly an encouragement of mid-day drinking at a professional meeting." Evening events also included free bars, he said.

The condoning of drinking at conventions results from ignorance, Cuellar said. "I'm not sure that folks in these organizations really understand the nature of the problem," he continued. "They tend to think of it as a problem of alcoholism, the dysfunctional alcoholic, rather than thinking about the problem of people who are alcohol dependent."[29]

During La Raza's three-day conference, Anheuser-Busch sponsored a welcoming reception and the opening luncheon; Coors sponsored an evening reception; Miller hosted a luncheon; Stroh Brewery paid for a dance; and Coca-Cola sponsored a reception. Coors, Coca-Cola, and Miller were "Golden Circle Sponsors," pitching in $15,000 each. "Silver Sponsors," at $10,000 each, were Anheuser-Busch and PepsiCo, and "Corporate Sponsors," contributing $5,000 each, in-

cluded Philip Morris and Stroh Brewery. Exhibitors included Anheuser-Busch, Coca-Cola, Coors, McDonald's, PepsiCo, RJR Nabisco,
and U.S. Tobacco Company.[30] The concurrent "Youth Leaders Program" for youths aged 15–19 included a dance sponsored by Stroh.

Raul Yzaguirre, La Raza's president, said the fact that alcohol and
tobacco companies sponsor conference events does not imply that La
Raza endorses the products. "What it says is that if you're a beer
drinker, consider in deciding which beer to drink the ones that have
been friendly to our community," he said. "I think that's all that it
says."

The level of involvement by alcohol and tobacco companies at
La Raza's convention is far from unique to that particular group. At
the 1988 convention of National IMAGE, a Hispanic group devoted to
education and employment issues, Miller Brewing sponsored a dance
and a reception; Coors hosted a fiesta; Coca-Cola paid for a luncheon
and the delegate assembly; and Anheuser-Busch sponsored a gala
dance. Full-page ads in the convention program were purchased by
Anheuser-Busch, Philip Morris, Coca-Cola, PepsiCo, Stroh, Miller
Brewing, and Coors.[31] Corporations pay between $12,000 and $25,000
to sponsor an event at the convention. That amount buys a lot of
things you'd expect: a full-color, full-page ad in the program; two ads
in the exhibitor directory; a convention banner with corporate logo;
ten registrations to the convention; "choice selection" of up to six
exhibit booths; and a reserved table at the sponsored event. But the
sponsorship also buys some things you might not expect. For example, the sponsor has the right to approve all the activities that take
place at its event. Sponsors also are invited to participate as "pre-
senters, panelists, and planners at workshops with visibility and
recognition in each workshop participating (sic)."[32]

Hispanic groups vary tremendously in the amount of general and
program support they receive from the alcohol, tobacco, and junk-
food companies. One major recipient is the Congressional Hispanic
Caucus Institute in Washington, D.C., which focuses primarily on
fellowship opportunities for high school and college students. Hispanic members of Congress created the Institute in 1978 and sit on its
board, but the Institute gets all of its funding from corporations and
the Ford Foundation.

In 1989 the Institute will receive at least $65,000 from the tobacco
industry, including RJR Nabisco, Philip Morris, U.S. Tobacco, and the
Tobacco Institute, according to Beverly Vigil Ellerman, the Institute's
executive director. Donations from Anheuser-Busch, Stroh Brewery,

Miller, and Coors are expected to total about $80,000. In addition, McDonald's will give about $70,000; Coke $50,000; and PepsiCo, which includes Pepsi and its fast-food divisions such as Pizza Hut and Taco Bell, will give $50,000. All told, alcohol, tobacco, and fast-food companies will contribute about $315,000 to the Institute, or nearly half of the $700,000 in corporate donations expected in 1989, Ellerman said.

Ellerman said the companies are now looking for substantive programs before they'll contribute. "In the last year to 18 months, there's a strong sense among these sorts of corporations to find real credible and productive kinds of programs where they think they can have a real impact on the community," she said. "They're not happy anymore just letting an organization have money to throw a party." However, the corporations do still contribute to the Institute's annual fundraising dinner.[33]

It's impossible to compile a complete list of all the contributions made to Hispanic organizations by alcohol, tobacco, and junk-food companies, but the following examples illustrate the range of activities supported:

- In the past, Anheuser-Busch helped finance LULAC's health fairs, where the company's sponsorship was prominently displayed.[34]

- Miller Brewing gave the U.S. Hispanic Chamber of Commerce $100,000 to open a Los Angeles regional office; Anheuser-Busch gave the same amount for an office in Washington, D.C.[35]

- RJR Nabisco gave the U.S. Hispanic Chamber $20,000 to publish the 1989 *National Hispanic Business Directory*.[36]

- The Coca-Cola Foundation and Coca-Cola USA gave the National Council of La Raza a $150,000 grant for community-based education projects.[37]

- The *Political Education Manual* published by LULAC contains an introduction written by the president of Philip Morris, which helped sponsor the publication.[38]

- Miller Brewing gave the U.S. Hispanic Chamber money to produce a film titled "Hispanic Business: A Force for the 80s."[39]

- Anheuser-Busch gave $20,000 to the Cuban American National Council for its Hispanic Leadership Development Training Seminar.[40]

- The director of public affairs for Burger King and a McDonald's franchisee are directors of the Cuban American National Council.[41] Corporate sponsors of the Council's 1988 convention included Adolph Coors, Miller Brewing, Anheuser-Busch, PepsiCo, and Schieffelin & Somerset (Johnnie Walker scotch, Hennessy cognac).[42] Both Burger King and Philip Morris participated in past conventions.[43]

- Corporate sponsors of SER - Jobs for Progress, a Hispanic organization devoted primarily to education and employment issues, have included Anheuser-Busch, Frito-Lay, McDonald's, PepsiCo, and Joseph E. Seagram & Sons.[44]
- Anheuser-Busch funds the policy analyst programs in Washington, D.C., California, and Texas of the Mexican American Legal Defense and Educational Fund (MALDEF).[45] Other contributors to MALDEF include Coca-Cola, Miller Brewing, and the Joseph Seagram and Sons, Inc. Fund.[46]
- Anheuser-Busch contributed $1 million to the National Hispanic Scholarship Fund in the form of advertising support and direct scholarship aid.[47]

Most of the contributions obviously support worthwhile programs, many of which would not happen without funding from the disease-promoting companies. Yet some Hispanic leaders are still leery about accepting alcohol and tobacco money. "I think it's great that you have a scholarship fund that is funded by Anheuser-Busch," said Torres. "But at the same time, we know that we're consuming their beer. Is that even? Is there as much negative as there is positive?"

Whether or not Hispanic organizations have been influenced by contributions from alcohol and tobacco companies, the fact remains that the national groups have not responded vigorously to the growing alcohol and smoking problems in the Hispanic community. "I think that all of our major organizations have been slow in moving in this area," said Bonilla, a failure he attributed to the lack of recognition by the general Hispanic community of the magnitude of alcohol and drug problems until the early 1980s.

The national organizations also haven't addressed health issues because of the numerous priorities in the Hispanic community, Bonilla said. "The nature of these problems of Hispanic America have been so diverse and so great that the emphasis has been on education and economic problems," he said. "Yet on the other hand, there's nothing more important to us than having a workforce not only that is educated but also that has a sound mind and sound body. And it's going to be hard to achieve that if you have alcohol and drug abuse prevalent in our society."

Yet another complicating factor has been the lack of good research on the extent of health problems facing the Hispanic community. "Not having the stats made it difficult for us to make the assertion of special interest in health issues," said Yzaguirre, the La Raza president. "But that's changing as we get more facts and figures."

The only major national Hispanic organizations with a significant focus on health is the National Coalition of Hispanic Health and Human Services Organizations (COSSMHO). Yet even COSSMHO received a $4,500 grant from Anheuser-Busch in 1988 to purchase computers.[48] However, COSSMHO recently adopted a new policy of not accepting funding from alcohol companies, according to Jane Delgado, president and chief executive officer, to go along with its previous policy of not accepting money from tobacco companies.[49] Delgado is still a member of the advisory committee of the National Hispana Leadership Initiative, a leadership training program for Hispanic women sponsored by Coors.

The Case of Coors

By the early 1980s, the Adolph Coors Co. was in serious trouble. While the Colorado brewer's biggest competitors—Anheuser-Busch and Miller Brewing—had undertaken massive marketing campaigns, Coors was caught sitting on its hands. In addition, Coors' plans to expand eastward from its western base were thwarted by a collection of groups ranging from Hispanic organizations to labor unions, which were boycotting Coors because of the company's antipathy toward minorities and its lousy labor relations.

The boycott's impact was devastating. In the key California market, for example, an alliance between the AFL-CIO and various Hispanic groups caused Coors' market share to plummet from 43 percent in 1977 to 14 percent in 1984.[50] Coors' market share was also suffering nationwide, dropping from a high of 7.6 percent in 1980 to 7.0 percent in 1984.[51] The result: Net profits in 1984 dropped more than 30 percent from 1980.[52]

The problems at Coors caused some to predict the brewer's demise. At the same time, several national Hispanic organizations were running into serious financial problems of their own. Thus was born a marriage of convenience.

In October 1984, Coors and seven national Hispanic organizations signed an agreement under which Coors promised to increase hiring of Hispanics, purchases from Hispanic suppliers, spending on Hispanic advertising, and sales of distributorships to Hispanics. The company also agreed to conduct a certain percentage of its business with Hispanic-owned banks, investment firms, and insurance companies. And finally, it agreed to contribute $500,000 per year to non-profit Hispanic organizations, with one-third targeted to educational programs. (That might sound like a lot of money, but to a large brewer it's equivalent to the cost of a few prime-time TV commercials.)

In return, the organizations agreed to "assist in increasing the understanding of Coors and its products within the Hispanic community... The Coalition [of Hispanic groups] will take positive and visible action to help eliminate misconceptions of Coors within the Hispanic community," according to the agreement.[53] The pact was signed by the National Council of La Raza, National IMAGE, the American G.I. Forum, LULAC, the U.S. Hispanic Chamber of Com-

Adolph Coors Company's campaign to win the hearts of Hispanics is also winning Coors' way into their pocketbooks. Advertising, donations, and business investments have led to higher beer sales.

merce, the Cuban National Planning Council, and the National Puerto Rican Coalition. However, the Puerto Rican Coalition pulled out of the agreement a few months later because of internal dissension.

Much of that dissension centered on a provision in the agreement that called for the Hispanic groups to help Coors "address ongoing issues and potential political and social difficulties that may occur in the national scene regarding Coors and its products."[54] Coors tried to insert the same provision in a pact it was negotiating at the same time with Black groups, but the Black organizations insisted that it be removed. An NAACP official told *Hispanic Business*, "We are not going to be a political buffer for Coors, nor are we going to market their products."[55]

Raul Yzaguirre, president of the National Council of La Raza and chief negotiator of the Hispanic agreement, said the buffer clause "was a very innocuous phrase." The clause was removed a few months after the agreement was signed because of criticism in the Hispanic community, he said.[56]

When the pact was signed, Coors said the five-year agreement would provide $350 million in benefits to the Hispanic community, a figure that is widely believed to be greatly exaggerated. Even Jerry Apodaca, who is in charge of monitoring Coors' compliance with the agreement, called the $350 million figure "an arbitrary number to some degree."[57]

Almost immediately, Coors started reaping the benefits of the pact. Hispanics accounted for just 5.6 percent of Coors' volume in 1984, the year the agreement was signed, but that figure jumped to nine percent by 1986.[58] Put another way, Hispanics accounted for $118.3 million in sales in 1986, up dramatically from $63.4 million in 1984.[59]

Hispanic leaders who negotiated the covenant say their community also has benefited. "Nowhere before had there been such a level of commitment from one company to a particular ethnic group," said Yzaguirre. "It was historic, it was groundbreaking. It set the pattern and it brought us together."[60]

One of the pact's most controversial provisions ties Coors' spending levels in many areas to increased consumption of Coors beer by Hispanics. "I greatly objected to the undeclared proposition that depending on how intoxicated you get the Hispanics will determine how much help we'll give the Hispanics," said Tony Bonilla, LULAC's former president and current chairman of the National Hispanic Leadership Conference.[61]

A paper by Dr. Raul Caetano in the *Report of the Secretary's Task Force on Black and Minority Health*, published by the U.S. Department of Health and Human Services, also criticized the linking of benefit levels to consumption. The link "means that Hispanic organizations involved in this plan have become partners of Coors in its attempt to increase alcohol consumption among Hispanics," the paper said.[62]

Rodolfo Acuna, a professor of Chicano studies at California State University-Northridge, wrote in a column in the *Los Angeles Herald Examiner* that critics of the agreement had coined a new motto for the Chicano movement: "Drink a Coors for La Raza!"[63]

Yzaguirre, the chief negotiator of the pact, said in a magazine interview that the signatories didn't expect the "incentive commitment" to be a problem.[64] "We had no notion that we were going to make alcoholics out of anybody," he said. "We were totally surprised that this would cause any concern for some folks. Frankly, I think

Coors' pact with Hispanic groups has been highly controversial. Some leaders fear that the quest for Coors' donations is obscuring — and even contributing to — alcohol problems in the Hispanic community. Here are Coors' ad dollars at work on the Sabado Gigante *TV show.*

people were looking for ways to criticize the agreement."

In an interview for this report, Yzaguirre said benefit levels for most major planks of the agreement, such as employment levels and the amount of charitable contributions, are not tied to consumption. He also denied that the pact encourages increased consumption of beer. "My feeling is we're not influencing consumption," he said. "The best that can be said is that the people will switch from Heileman's or Beck's to Coors."[65]

But Bonilla, the former LULAC president, disagreed. "Whether that's what they intended, there's a perception that's been created and it's not a good perception," he said. "After all, one of the major problems facing the Hispanic community in America today is alcohol and drug abuse. And when you have a written provision tying consumption into the trade agreement, it does harm to the efforts that are being made to combat alcoholism in our community."

Some Hispanic leaders are quite forthright in describing their interest in having the pact succeed. "The Hispanic community has a vested interest in having the company succeed," said Hector Barreto, the former president of the U.S. Hispanic Chamber of Commerce and a signatory to the agreement. "If the company doesn't succeed, there ain't no way we can collect."[66]

Those who signed the agreement say they have maintained their objectivity and held Coors accountable. Coors' compliance level with the agreement is "very high," according to Apodaca, who is in charge of monitoring Coors' compliance with the agreement. The company has done particularly well in procurement from Hispanic companies, he said. Coors bought about $1.6 million in goods from a small number of Hispanic suppliers in 1984, he said, but now annually buys more than $20 million in goods from more than 600 Hispanic vendors.

Of course, Apodaca has a vested interest in putting the best possible light on the Coors agreement. That's because Coors provided 100 percent of the funding for HACER, including Apodaca's salary, when the group was first founded, and continues to provide significant funding today.

Yzaguirre, the primary negotiator of the Coors agreement, downplayed Coors' funding of HACER. "The money you're talking about is minuscule," he said. "At first it was 100 percent of what we had, but in total dollars it was rather minuscule. I think they gave us $30,000 or $40,000 the first year, and now it's $30,000 and going down every year. And our total budget now is about $100,000."[67]

Coors also is doing well in meeting the agreement's goals on

Soft-sell ads like this one for an exhibit of Hispanic art are part of Coors' and other companies' efforts to improve their image and sales in the Hispanic community.

advertising and banking, Apodaca said. The company has done "reasonably well" in meeting employment goals, he said, although it has not met the commitment for moving Hispanics into higher-level positions in the company. The goal of adding 20 new Hispanic distributors also is far from being met, Apodaca said. The company has only awarded a few Hispanic distributorships so far, and two of those went to Los Angeles Raiders quarterback Jim Plunkett and former coach Tom Flores, Hispanics who aren't exactly fighting their way out of the barrio.[68]

One goal Coors has made sure it met is the commitment to contribute at least $500,000 per year to non-profit Hispanic organizations. A partial listing of Hispanic groups that got funding from Coors in 1987–88 includes:

Association for the Advancement of Mexican-Americans
Council of Hispanic Young Professionals and Students
Cuban American National Council
Cuban National Planning Council
Cuban Professional Journalist Association
Hispanic Alliance for Career Enhancement
Hispanic Association on Corporate Responsibility
U.S. Hispanic Chamber of Commerce
Hispanic National Bar Association
Latin American Bar Association
Latin American Police Association
Latin Business and Professional Women's Club
Latin Chamber of Commerce of the U.S.A.
League of United Latin American Citizens (LULAC)
National Council of La Raza
National Hispanic University
Organization of Spanish-Speaking Officers
Puerto Rican Society of Waukegan
Society of Hispanic Professional Engineers
Spanish Coalition for Jobs
United Puerto Rican Parade Committee[69]

Philanthropy: A Look to the Future

If Hispanic organizations are ever to free themselves of the entanglements caused by alcohol and tobacco money, new sources of funds must be found. Philanthropic foundations and companies that produce safe products must be far more generous than they have been in the past. The government programs and grants that assisted many Hispanic (and other minority) organizations need to be revived. Unfortunately, all this is easier said than done.

One alternative increasingly being discussed in the Hispanic community is to turn to the community itself for support. Rejecting the pathogenic corporations and depending on the community for support would ultimately strengthen the Hispanic society, said Arnoldo Torres, national political director of LULAC. "If we could somehow begin to have our own community contribute some of that money that they in fact use to buy those products, and turn it into a self-help effort. . .then we basically would not need the contributions from them," he said. "In fact, we would probably do even better if we could be able to get that type of social consciousness coming out of our community."

Change will come slowly, but frank discussion of the pervasive influence of the alcoholic-beverage, tobacco, and junk-food industries on the Hispanic community is a necessary first step. In an effort to give greater specificity to that debate, we present several conclusions and recommendations in the next chapter.

6

Conclusions and Recommendations

I n this report we have documented the pervasive and growing influence of alcohol, tobacco, soft-drink, and fast-food companies in the Hispanic community. Of course, those same companies also are omnipresent in the general American society, peddling their oftentimes-harmful products at every possible opportunity.

But promotions of alcohol, tobacco, soft drinks, and fast foods targeted at Hispanics deserve special scrutiny, since large numbers of Hispanics are particularly vulnerable to diseases caused by those products. Special attention also is dictated by the fact that poor health practices such as heavy drinking and eating of large quantities of fried food are relatively common in the Hispanic community.

Up to now, little attention has been focused on Hispanic health concerns by the federal government or medical researchers. The result is that our knowledge about Hispanic health problems and their causes is woefully inadequate. Even such basic information as the prevalence of smoking or drinking does not exist for many of the Hispanic sub-groups. And while basic data is available for sub-groups such as Mexican-Americans, no definitive information exists about what causes practices like heavy drinking by Mexican-American men. Without such basic information, it's difficult to design effective prevention and treatment programs.

Both the government and researchers have taken a greater interest in Hispanic health issues in the last few years. For example, the National Cancer Institute is funding smoking prevention and cessation projects directed at Hispanics in a handful of cities around the country. But after years of neglect, many needs are still unmet.

Some of the neglect has occurred because the major national Hispanic organizations have been largely silent about health issues affecting their community. In some ways it is hard to fault them, since there have been so many pressing priorities facing the Hispanic community, such as education, housing, jobs, and the acquisition of political rights.

And yet children in a Hispanic family that is kept in constant chaos by the father's drinking problem stand little chance of succeeding in school. And Hispanics who die prematurely from lung cancer caused by smoking have their political rights buried with them.

Health concerns cannot be separated from other issues in the Hispanic community. For example, it's sheer folly to try to solve the alarming school dropout problem — Hispanic high-school students have higher drop-out rates[1] than either Blacks or Whites — without taking into account the increasing use of alcohol and other substances by Hispanic teenagers. Ignoring the health problems in the community only makes it that much harder to solve other problems that the community faces.

Some national Hispanic groups have recently initiated AIDS projects to educate members of their communities, which have been particularly hard hit by the disease. Such projects are clearly commendable. But all too many of these same organizations continue to ignore the terrible ravaging of their communities by alcohol and tobacco, a ravaging that is killing far more of their people than AIDS will ever claim. Why these groups have ignored alcohol and tobacco issues is undoubtedly related in part to the tens of thousands of dollars they receive annually in contributions from alcohol and tobacco companies.

But, in addition, many Hispanic leaders may have avoided health concerns related to alcohol, tobacco, and junk foods largely out of ignorance of the enormous impact these substances are having on their communities. For example, in interviewing numerous Hispanic leaders we found that few were aware of the seriousness of the alcohol-abuse problem among Hispanics. One nationally-respected leader said he had never seen a study indicating that Hispanics suffered from greater alcohol-abuse problems than the general population. As we documented earlier in this report, however, numerous such studies exist.

Today, targeted advertising and other promotional efforts by the alcohol, tobacco, fast-food, and soft-drink industries seriously endanger the health of millions of Hispanics. If the health problems associated with these products are to be reduced, certain actions must be taken. The following recommendations are offered to government, producers of the disease-promoting products, businesses of all types, and the national Hispanic organizations.

The government should:

- Increase funding for research into health problems in the Hispanic community either caused or exacerbated by alcohol, tobacco, and fatty, sugary foods. Such research should determine the prevalence of health problems related to those products, the rate of use of those products, and why some Hispanic sub-groups use those products at greater rates than other sub-groups or the general population. Research also should examine the marketing and advertising of disease-promoting products. The research results should be widely disseminated among Hispanic leaders and the general public.

- Increase funding for prevention and treatment programs aimed at heavy drinkers and smokers in the Hispanic community.

- Enact and enforce zoning laws to control the distribution and operation of new and existing alcohol outlets in Hispanic neighborhoods to reduce proliferation, undue concentration, and their placement in high-risk environments.

- Enact laws to restrict or ban billboards so that Hispanic areas are not besieged by a disproportionate number of alcohol and tobacco billboards. Many cities and four states (Alaska, Hawaii, Maine, Vermont) have banned all billboards.

- Greatly increase funding for jobs, education, health, and other programs that are vitally needed in the Hispanic community.

Producers of alcoholic beverages, cigarettes, and potentially harmful foods should:

- Voluntarily limit billboard advertising in areas of dense minority population so that it does not exceed levels of advertising in White, middle-class neighborhoods. Each billboard ad also should be matched, or alternated, with health messages.

- Fund comprehensive community education and prevention programs to help reduce problems caused by alcohol, tobacco, and poor nutrition in Hispanic communities. Hispanic media and advertising agencies also should contribute to these programs.

- Stop tying economic assistance to increased consumption of their products by Hispanics.

- Reduce the alcohol content of malt liquor and stop targeting Hispanics (and Blacks) with ads for those products.

Businesses of all types should:

- Increase advertising in Hispanic media and contributions to Hispanic groups. Such actions would respond to a social need, create goodwill and sales, and reduce the dependence of Hispanic media and organizations on contributions from disease-promoting companies.

National Hispanic organizations should:

- Make health promotion and disease prevention a top priority for their organizations and affiliates around the country.

- Initiate programs to educate their members and the Hispanic community about the special health risks that alcohol, tobacco, and fatty, sugary foods pose for Hispanics.

- Support and encourage locally-based alcohol and smoking prevention and treatment programs around the country.

- Take the lead in pressuring state and federal governments to devote additional resources to the health problems of the Hispanic community.

- Consider whether their acceptance of money from alcohol and tobacco companies makes it difficult for them to properly tackle health problems. If possible, they should attempt to gradually replace donations from the alcohol and tobacco companies with other money, such as donations from the increasingly populous and wealthy Hispanic community itself.

In addition to developing or expanding programs geared specifically to Hispanics, government at the local, state, and national levels should undertake a wide variety of other activities that would benefit society at large. These include such things as:

- Raising excise taxes on alcoholic beverages and cigarettes, and using some of the increased revenues for health programs.

- Prohibiting the sale of cigarettes from vending machines, which are freely available to children.
- Banning all advertising for alcoholic beverages and cigarettes that link those products to health, youthfulness, and vigor.
- Improving the quality of meals served in schools, and expanding nutrition education programs.

It's obvious that the disease-promoting companies care enough about profits from the Hispanic community to spend millions of dollars trying to hook Hispanics on their products. Now the question is whether government, other businesses, and Hispanic organizations themselves care enough to take the actions necessary to help the youthful, fast-growing Hispanic community thrive and prosper.

BEEFEATER® GIN
Se distingue claramente.

Beefeater tiene un sabor perfectamente balanceado, suave, seco...
de carácter extraordinario. Saboréelo con naranja, toronja,
tónico...con lo que sea.

Después de todo, cuando usted toma Beefeater, se distingue claramente.

Afterword

Rodolfo Acuña, Ph.D.
Professor of Chicano Studies,
California State University, Northridge

Juana Mora, Ph.D.
Research Analyst
Los Angeles County Office of Alcohol Programs

The Mexican revolutionary — with a push from the Mexican and American film industries — has come to symbolize a man with a pistol in one hand and a bottle of tequila in the other. This invented tradition of the *macho* has also been exaggerated by popular Mexican culture, making the drinking of alcohol synonymous with being a "man." This phenomenon has created a permissiveness toward alcohol use encouraging the spread of an epidemic within our community that contradicts the values espoused by the Mexican Revolution and the virtues of the Mexican family.

The crisis proportions of alcohol and other sources of consumer abuse among Latinos in the United States makes works such as *Marketing Disease to Hispanics* vital in the war against the alcohol, tobacco, and fast-food industries' conscious campaign to addict Third World communities inside and outside the borders of the First World.

The report from the Center for Science in the Public Interest synthesizes the scant literature in the field. Given the magnitude of the problem, one would expect the health community and Latino activists to have paid more attention. The report itself makes excellent use of existing studies to underscore the pattern of abuse both by the users and the peddlers. Clearly, the conclusion is that, with the growing health consciousness of the White middle-class, the peddlers have turned to the Third World, at home and abroad, to maintain and increase their profits.

The devastation caused by alcohol alone is stunning. Alcohol use among Whites is generally a problem of the young, whereas Mexican-American males drink excessively while young and keep on drinking into middle and older ages. Among men, the rate of death from alcoholism is twice as great among Mexican-Americans as Whites. And Mexican-Americans have a higher rate of arrests and imprisonment for intoxication than the general population.

The report also deals with tobacco and junk foods. In a nutshell, the rate of lung cancer among Latinos has been increasing at a higher rate than among Euro-Americans. The tobacco industry has followed the lead of the liquor companies: It heavily markets its drug at Latino celebrations, and its billboards pollute the barrios.

The report cites surveys that indicate that Latinos consume more fast food and cola drinks than other groups. Those foods are loaded with fat, calories, and sugar. Consequently, between cirrhosis of the liver, lung cancer, and hardening of the arteries, the casualties in the Latino community promise to grow.

As in other forms of environmental racism, Latinos are singled out and targeted by greedy business interests that play to the weaknesses in our culture that permit and even celebrate the use of alcohol and tobacco. The use of the cultural information by the industry to reinforce a pattern of consumption leading to abuse and health problems is not marketing, but intentional victimization of a group of people who are poor, different, and vulnerable.

The truth be told, there is a conscious movement by the big 3 to shift the blame to the victims by suggesting that alcohol, tobacco, and junk-food abuse is an individual choice. As in the case of other drugs and pornography, the line is "just say no," but here companies aim millions of dollars of slick advertising at adults and children to use their product. This is no solution.

We must turn the symbol of the Mexican Revolutionary from that of the *bironga* (beer) to the "book." We must first educate ourselves about the alcohol, tobacco, and fast-food crisis and then spread the word. Spanish-language radio, television, and magazines (in particular) need to be enlisted in this process.

The solution to the health crisis in Third World communities is not individual. That will only result in putting more Latinos in jail. The solution is in countering the hegemony of the big 3, creating a mindset where abuse is not tolerated, snickered at, or even celebrated. We must become intolerant and react to the marketers of alcohol, tobacco, and fast food in the same way that we do to those who overtly call us greasers.

It is time that we take the lead in criticizing our national organizations, civic leaders, and elected officials for promoting disease. These groups and individuals openly take money from the tobacco and liquor industries without addressing cigarette and alcohol use as major public health issues in our communities. The infamous Coors deal — where our most respected organizations (American G.I.

Forum, LULAC, and other Latino groups) called off a boycott of Coors beer and, in fact, became Coors sponsors — is not unique. All such deals are tied to the increased consumption of alcohol and tobacco by poor Latinos.

Elected officials and grassroots groups are mute on the beer companies taking over the 5 *de Mayo* and the "16th of September" celebrations. In private they argue that getting money from beer and tobacco companies is the only way they can raise the money that they need to serve the community. They also reason that the beer companies are giving distributorships and jobs to Latinos. And how can you argue against affirmative action?

Well, Latinos *should* argue against affirmative action when the result is detrimental to the general welfare of the community, in the same way we have fought developers who want to bulldoze entire communites for profit. What does it matter if the developer is Black, White, or Brown? What does it matter if the pusher is of your same race?

The time has come for a national debate among Latinos on the question of all three forms of product targeting to Latinos. Solutions have to go beyond just saying no and having the pushers of alcohol and tobacco pay for an occasional public service message about the disease that they profit from.

We must support public policies that promote a reduced number of liquor stores in our communities, stricter enforcement of sales to minors, restrictions on advertising in English and Spanish media, and higher alcohol and tobacco taxes. Studies show that an increase in taxes reduces consumption, so let's stop the sophistry and tell the people who talk about the unfair taxing of the poor to shut up! Let's raise the taxes and then demand that our community gets its proportional share of the increased tax revenues.

For our own sake, the Latino community has to end the domination by the beer and tobacco companies that for the past twenty years have written our history through the production of their calendars, radio and TV commercials, magazine ads, donations to civic groups, and other forms of influence. The dependency of our community organizations and elected officials on beer and tobacco revenue is dangerous. And it can no longer be rationalized. We cannot go back to the early 1970s when many said that they were selling drugs to subsidize the movement. It was a *pendejada* (stupidity) then, and it is a *pendejada* today. We must take a stand.

NOTES

Foreword

1. Telephone interview, March 9, 1989.

Chapter 1. Marketers Discover Hispanics (pages 1-5)

1. Edward Simmen, *Pain & Promise: The Chicano Today* (New York: New American Library, 1972), p. 94.

2. Joan Moore and Harry Pachon, *Hispanics in the United States* (Englewood Cliffs: Prentice-Hall, 1985), p. 9.

3. "Sí, Pepsi Habla Español," *USA Today,* Feb. 21, 1989, p. 2B.

4. U.S., Department of Commerce, Bureau of the Census, *The Hispanic Population in the United States: March 1988 (Advance Report),* Current Population Reports Series P-20, No. 431 (Washington, D.C.: Government Printing Office, 1988), p. 1.

5. "Out of the Barrio and Into the Mainstream," *The New York Times,* June 26, 1988.

6. U.S., Department of Commerce, Bureau of the Census, *Projections of the Hispanic Population: 1983 to 2080,* Current Population Reports, Series P-25, No. 995 (Washington, D.C.: Government Printing Office, 1986), p. 10.

7. U.S., Department of Census, *The Hispanic Population,* p. 1.

8. Ibid, p. 7.

9. U.S., Department of Commerce, *Projections of the Hispanic Population,* p. 2.

10. Humberto Valencia, "Hispanic Purchasing Power on the Rise," *Hispanic Business,* December 1988, p. 22.

11. "Advertisers Make Pitch for Hispanics," *USA Today,* Oct. 7, 1987, p. 1.

12. "Hispanic Markets: Future is Fabuloso," *Adweek,* Dec. 1, 1986.

13. Pete Engardio, "Fast Times on Avenida Madison," *Business Week,* June 6, 1988.

14. "Seekers of Hispanic Markets Find a Helpful Tool: English," *The New York Times,* June 13, 1988, p. D9.

15. Telephone interview, March 13, 1989.

16. D. Carlos Balkan, "Corporate Ad Spending Takes A Dive," *Hispanic Business,* December 1988, p. 19.

17. Ibid.

18. "Hispanic Market Booms, Marketers Take Notice," *Boston Globe,* July 31, 1988.

19. "Demand for Hispanic Ads Outstrips Specialists in Field," *The Wall Street Journal,* June 29, 1989, p. B1.

Chapter 2. Hispanic Health Risks (pages 7-26).

1. Kyriakos S. Markides and Jeannine Coreil, "The Health of Hispanics in the Southwestern United States: an Epidemiologic Paradox," *Public Health Reports,* May-June 1986, p. 262.

2. Anthony M. Alcocer, "Alcohol Use and Abuse Among the Hispanic American Population." In National Institute on Alcohol Abuse and Alcoholism, *Special Population Issues*, Alcohol and Health Monograph No. 4 (Washington D.C.: Government Printing Office, 1982), p. 375.

3. Telephone interview, March 6, 1989.

4. M. Jean Gilbert and Richard C. Cervantes, "Alcohol Services for Mexican Americans: A Review of Utilization Patterns, Treatment Considerations and Prevention Activities," *Hispanic Journal of Behavioral Sciences*, Vol. 8, No. 3, 1986, p. 192.

5. Telephone interview, March 8, 1989.

6. Arleen Rogan, "Alcohol and Ethnic Minorities: Hispanics—An Update," Reprint from *Alcohol Health & Research World*, National Clearinghouse for Alcohol Information, undated, p. 7.

7. Raul Caetano, "Drinking Patterns and Alcohol Problems in a National Sample of U.S. Hispanics." Paper presented at the National Institute on Alcohol Abuse and Alcoholism Conference, *Epidemiology of Alcohol Use and Abuse Among U.S. Ethnic Minorities*, Bethesda, Md., 1985, p. 1.

8. Raul Caetano, "Ethnicity and Drinking in Northern California: A Comparison among Whites, Blacks and Hispanics," *Alcohol & Alcoholism*, Vol. 19, No. 1, 1984, p. 33.

9. M. Jean Gilbert and Richard Cervantes, "Patterns and Practices of Alcohol Use Among Mexican Americans: A Comprehensive Review," *Hispanic Journal of Behavioral Sciences*, Vol. 8, No. 1, 1986, p. 29.

10. Raul Caetano, "Drinking and Hispanic-American Family Life: The View Outside the Clinic Walls," *Alcohol Health and Research World*, Winter 1986/87, p. 28.

11. Cited in Gilbert and Cervantes, "Patterns and Practices of Alcohol Use," p. 29.

12. Ibid.

13. U.S., Department of Health and Human Services, *Report of the Secretary's Task Force on Black and Minority Health*, (Washington, D.C.: Government Printing Office, 1985), Vol. I, p. 78.

14. Alcocer, "Alcohol Use and Abuse," p. 368, and Gilbert and Cervantes, "Patterns and Practices of Alcohol Use," p. 26.

15. Alcocer, "Alcohol Use and Abuse," p. 368.

16. Gilbert and Cervantes, "Alcohol Services for Mexican Americans," p. 216.

17. Ibid, p. 197.

18. Kyriakos Markides, Neal Krause, Carlos Mendes de Leon, "Accultura-

tion and Alcohol Consumption Among Mexican Americans: A Three-Generation Study," *American Journal of Public Health*, September 1988, p. 1179.

19. Caetano, "Drinking Patterns and Alcohol Problems," p. 2.

20. Caetano, "Ethnicity and Drinking in Northern California," p. 36.

21. Gilbert and Cervantes, "Patterns and Practices of Alcohol Use," p. 27.

22. Telephone interview, Feb. 28, 1989.

23. Cited in Gilbert and Cervantes, "Patterns and Practices of Alcohol Use," p. 29.

24. Raul Caetano, "Patterns and Problems of Drinking Among U.S. Hispanics." In *Report of the Secretary's Task Force*, Vol. VII, p. 161.

25. Caetano, "Ethnicity and Drinking in Northern California," p. 39.

26. Telephone interview, Feb. 28, 1989.

27. Caetano, "Ethnicity and Drinking in Northern California," p. 34.

28. Caetano, "Drinking and Hispanic-American Family Life," p. 26.

29. Gilbert and Cervantes, "Patterns and Practices of Alcohol Use," p. 46.

30. Ibid., p. 47.

31. Markides, Krause and Mendes de Leon, "Acculturation and Alcohol Consumption," p. 1181.

32. Ames and Mora, "Alcohol Problem Prevention," p. 7.

33. Raul Caetano, personal communication, May 9, 1989.

34. Rogan, "Alcohol and Ethnic Minorities," p. 7.

35. Telephone interview, Feb. 28, 1989.

36. Ames and Mora, "Alcohol Problem Prevention," p. 22.

37. Cited in Antonio Estrada, Jerome Rabow, and Ronald Watts, "Alcohol Use Among Hispanic Adolescents: A Preliminary Report," *Hispanic Journal of Behavioral Sciences*, Vol. 4, No. 3, 1982, p. 341.

38. Alfred Marcus and Lori Crane, "Smoking Behavior Among Hispanics: A Preliminary Report." In *Advances in Cancer Control: Epidemiology and Research* (New York: Alan R. Liss, 1984), p. 145.

39. U.S., Department of Health and Human Services, *Report of the Secretary's Task Force on Black and Minority Health*, Vol. III, p. 22.

40. Cited in Alfred Marcus and Lori Crane, "Smoking Behavior Among U.S. Latinos: An Emerging Challenge for Public Health," *American Journal of Public Health*, February 1985, p. 170.

41. Cited in "Cigarettes: Still Big Business," *The New York Times*, June 12, 1988.

42. Patrick Remington, Michele Forman, Eileen Gentry, James Marks, Gary Hogelin, and Frederick Trowbridge, "Current Smoking Trends in the United States: The 1981-83 Behavioral Risk Factor Surveys," *Journal of the American Medical Association*, May 24/31, 1985, p. 2977.

43. Luís Escobedo and Patrick Remington, "Birth Cohort Analysis of Prevalence of Cigarette Smoking Among Hispanics in the United States," *Journal of the American Medical Association*, Jan. 6, 1989, p. 69.

44. Telephone interview, March 2, 1989.

45. Telephone inteview, March 9, 1989.

46. Cited in Marcus and Crane, "Smoking Behavior Among U.S. Latinos," p. 171.

47. David Savitz, "Changes in Spanish Surname Cancer Rates Relative to Other Whites, Denver Area, 1969-71 to 1979-81," *American Journal of Public Health*, October 1986, p. 1212.

48. Jonathan Samet, Charles Wiggins, Charles Key, and Thomas Becker, "Mortality from Lung Cancer and Chronic Obstructive Pulmonary Disease in New Mexico, 1958-1982," *American Journal of Public Health*, September 1988, p. 1183.

49. Ibid.

50. Marcus and Crane, "Smoking Behavior Among Hispanics," p. 149.

51. Richard Rogers and John Crank, "Ethnic Differences in Smoking Patterns: Findings from NHIS," *Public Health Reports*, July-August 1988, p. 391.

52. Telephone interview, March 21, 1989.

53. Kyriakos Markides, Jeannine Coreil, and Laura Ray, "Smoking Among Mexican Americans: A Three-Generation Study," *American Journal of Public Health*, June 1987, p. 710.

54. Claudia Baquet, "The Association of Tobacco to Cancer and Other Health Conditions in Minority Populations," National Cancer Institute, Division of Cancer Prevention and Control, unpublished, March 1987, p. 16.

55. *Report of the Secretary's Task Force*, Vol. III, p. 21.

56. Ibid., p. 22.

57. Savitz, "Changes in Spanish Surname Cancer Rates," p. 1212.

58. Telephone Interview, March 9, 1989.

59. Marcus and Crane, "Smoking Behavior," pp. 148-49.

60. Cited in *Report of the Secretary's Task Force,* Vol. VII, p. 35.

61. Margaret Greenberg, Charles Wiggins, Daniel Kutvirt, and Jonathan Samet, "Cigarette Use among Hispanic and Non-Hispanic White School Children, Albuquerque, New Mexico," *American Journal of Public Health*, May 1987, p. 621.

62. Ibid., p. 621.

63. Escobedo and Remington, "Birth Cohort Analysis," p. 67.

64. Felipe Castro, Lourdes Baezconde-Garbanati and Hector Beltran, "Risk Factors for Coronary Heart Disease in Hispanic Populations: A Review," *Hispanic Journal of Behavoral Sciences*, Vol. 7, No. 2, 1985, p. 168.

65. U.S., Department of Health and Human Services, Public Health Service, *The Surgeon General's Report on Nutrition and Health* (Washington, D.C.: Government Printing Office, 1988), p. 254.

66. National Research Council, *Diet and Health: Implications for Reducing Chronic Disease Risk* (Washington D.C.: National Academy Press, 1989), p. 24-2.

67. *The Surgeon General's Report on Nutrition and Health*, p. 258.

68. National Institutes of Health, "Diet and Exercise in Noninsulin-Depend-

ent Diabetes Mellitus," *Consensus Development Conference Statement*, Vol. 6, No. 8, 1986, p. 2.

69. National Coalition of Hispanic Health and Human Services Organizations, *Selected Population and Health Data Comparisons* (Washington, D.C., 1988), p. 9.

70. Markides and Coreil, "The Health of Hispanics in the Southwestern United States, p. 258.

71. *Diet and Health*, p. 5-44.

72. Michael Stern, "Factors Relating to the Increased Prevalence of Diabetes in Hispanic Americans." In *Report of the Secretary's Task Force,* Vol. VII, p. 360.

73. *The Surgeon General's Report on Nutrition and Health*, p. 255.

74. F.C. Wood and E.L. Bierman, "Is Diet the Cornerstone in Management of Diabetes?" *New England Journal of Medicine*, Vol. 315, 1986, pp. 1224-1227.

75. U.S. Department of Health, Education, and Welfare, *Report of the National Commission on Diabetes to the Congress of the United States, Vol. I: The Long Range Plan to Combat Diabetes* (Washington, D.C.: Government Printing Office, 1976), p. 2.

76. National Institutes of Health, "Diet and Exercise in Noninsulin-Dependent Diabetes Mellitus," p. 2.

77. A.H. Kissebah, N. Vydelingum, R. Murray, D.J. Evans, A.J. Hartz, R.K. Kalhoff, and P.W. Adams, "Relation of Body Fat Distribution to Metabolic Complications of Obesity," *Journal of Clinical Endocrinology and Metabolism*, Vol. 54, 1982, pp. 254-260.

78. S.M. Haffner, H.P. Stern, J. Hazuda, J. Pugh, and J.K. Patterson, "Do Upper-Body and Centralized Adiposity Measure Different Aspects of Regional Body-Fat Distribution? Relationship to Noninsulin-dependent Diabetes Mellitus, Lipids, and Lipoproteins," *Diabetes*, Vol. 36, 1987, pp. 43-51.

79. Castro, Baezconde-Garbanati, and Beltran, "Risk Factors for Coronary Heart Disease," pp. 163-164.

80. *Report of the Secretary's Task Force*, Vol. IV, Part 1, p. 68.

81. Deborah Dawson, "Ethnic Differences in Female Overweight: Data from the 1985 National Health Inteview Survey," *American Journal of Public Health*, October 1988, p. 1327.

82. National Institutes of Health, "Diet and Exercise in Noninsulin-Dependent Diabetes Mellitus," p. 3.

83. *The Surgeon General's Report on Nutrition and Health*, p. 255.

84. National Institutes of Health, "Diet and Exercise in Noninsulin-Dependent Diabetes Mellitus," p. 2.

85. Ibid.

86. American Diabetes Association Task Force on Nutrition and Exchange Lists, "Nutritional Recommendations and Principles for Individuals with Diabetes Mellitus," *Diabetes Care*, Vol. 10, 1987, pp. 126-132.

87. J.D. Brunzell, R.L. Lerner, W.R. Hazzard, D. Porte, and E.L. Bierman,

"Improved Glucose Tolerance with High Carbohydrate Feeding in Mild Diabetes," *New England Journal of Medicine*, Vol. 284, 1971, pp. 521-524.

88. Telephone interview, March 16, 1989.

89. National Institutes of Health, "Diet and Exercise in Noninsulin-Dependent Diabetes Mellitus," p. 4.

90. Pete Engardio, "Fast Times on Avenida Madison," *Business Week*, June 6, 1988.

91. "Hispanic Consumers Loyal to Fast-Food Chains," *Nation's Restaurant News*, April 3, 1989, p. 15.

92. Carol Wheelan, "Grassroots Efforts Grow," *Food and Beverage Marketing*, April 1987, p. 35.

93. *Report of the Secretary's Task Force*, Vol. IV, Part 1, p. 61.

Chapter 3. Targeting Hispanics (pages 27-46)

1. Telephone interview, March 13, 1989.

2. Telephone interview, March 14, 1989.

3. D. Carlos Balkan, "The Hispanic Market's Leading Indicators," *Hispanic Business*, December 1988, p. 26.

4. "Alcoholism—Severe Health Problem for Latinos," *Nuestro*, March 1982, p. 35.

5. "Heileman Unveils a Dry Malt Brew, Called Colt 45 Dry," *The Wall Street Journal*, March 29, 1989, p. B6.

6. Telephone interview, Feb. 27, 1989.

7. Bruce Nash and Allan Zullo, *The Mis-Fortune 500* (Pocket), p. 88.

8. Telephone interview, March 12, 1989.

9. Telephone interview, Feb. 28, 1989.

10. "Alcohol Promotions Target Hispanics," *Prevention File*, Winter 1989, p. 11.

11. Telephone inteview, March 8, 1989.

12. Telephone interview, March 15, 1989.

13. Coalition for Scenic Beauty (now Scenic America), "Fact Sheet: Alcohol and Tobacco Advertising on Billboards," undated, (Washington, D.C.).

14. Telephone interview, March 1, 1989.

15. Marc Kornblatt, "Targeting the Hispanic Market," *Liquor Store*, June 1985, p. 22.

16. Ibid., p. 25.

17. Pete Engardio, "Fast Times on Avenida Madison," *Business Week*, June 6, 1988.

18. "Spanish-Language TV Blooms," *The Miami Herald*, July 11, 1988.

19. Letter from Donald G. Raider, chief operating officer, Telemundo Group Inc., June 2, 1989.

20. Telephone interview, March 13, 1989.

21. Personal interview, Feb. 22, 1989.

22. "Can You Conga?" *Hispanic*, March 1989, p. 20.
23. Telephone interview, March 8, 1989.
24. Ronald Davis, "Current Trends in Cigarette Advertising and Marketing," *New England Journal of Medicine*, Vol. 316, No. 12, 1987, p. 730.
25. Nadine Epstein, "Sending Smoke Signals to Minorities," *American Medical News*, Dec. 9, 1988, p. 25.
26. "Seekers of Hispanic Markets Find a Helpful Tool: English," *The New York Times*, June 13, 1988, p. D9.
27. Telephone interview, March 9, 1989.
28. Telephone interview, March 16, 1989.
29. Telephone interview, March 15, 1989.
30. Telephone interview, March 1, 1989.
31. Telephone interview, March 2, 1989.
32. Telephone interview, March 17, 1989.
33. Telephone interview, March 16, 1989.
34. Telephone interview, March 13, 1989.
35. Telephone interview, March 15, 1989.
36. U.S., Public Health Service, *Reducing the Health Consequences of Smoking: 25 Years of Progress* (Washington, D.C.: Government Printing Office, 1989).
37. Telephone interview, March 17, 1989.
38. Susan Milligan, "Eyes on the Lies: How Black Leaders and Cigarette Companies Have Turned Indoor Smoking into a Civil Rights Issue," *Washington Monthly*, June 1987, p. 41.
39. Telephone interview, March 15, 1989.
40. "Sí, Pepsi Habla Español," *USA Today*, Feb. 21, 1989, p. 2B.
41. "Pepsi Finds Key to Promotions," *Advertising Age*, Dec. 28, 1987, p. 19, and "The Hispanic Generation," *Hispanic Business*, January 1988, p. 39.
42. Coca-Cola ad, *Hispanic Business*, June 1988, p. 17.
43. Pepsi ad, *Hispanic Business*, December 1987, p. 29.
44. PepsiCo ad, *SER America*, Spring 1988, p. 53.
45. Marilyn Alva, "Chains Commit More Ad Time to Growing Hispanic Market," *Nation's Restaurant News*, Feb. 22, 1988, p. 12.
46. Raymond Serafin, "Domino's Plans Hispanic Push: Applies McDonald's Tactic to Pizza," *Nation's Restaurant News*, Feb. 22, 1988, p. 12.
47. Cuban American National Council, "HACER-McDonald's Sign $200 Million Agreement," *The Council Letter*, Fall 1988, p. 1.
48. "You'll Always Be Our Baby," *Hispanic Business*, March 1988, p. 47.
49. McDonald's ad, *Hispanic Business*, February 1985, p. 11.
50. Personal interview, Feb. 22, 1989.
51. "Pizza Chain Awakens," *Hispanic Business*, October 1987, p. 46.
52. Alva, "Chains Commit More Ad Time."
53. Domino's Pizza ad, *Hispanic*, March 1988, p. 9.
54. Alva, "Chains Commit More Ad Time."

Chapter 4. Event Marketing (pages 47-53)

1. Telephone interview, March 16, 1989.
2. Telephone interview, March 8, 1989.
3. "Firms Target Hispanics on Cinco de Mayo," *USA Today*, May 2, 1988, p. B1.
4. "Trouble at Cinco de Mayo Events Could Doom Future Festivals," the *Los Angeles Times*, May 8, 1989, metro section, part II, p. 3.
5. Rodolfo Acuna, "Put Cinco de Mayo On the Wagon," *Los Angeles Herald Examiner*, May 15, 1987, p. A21.
6. American Management Association, *Successful Marketing to U.S. Hispanics and Asians: Players, Agencies, and Media* (New York: American Management Association, 1987), p. 24.
7. Liz Murphy, "The Controversy Behind Event Marketing," *Sales and Marketing Management*, October 1986, pp. 55-56.
8. "Winston Continues Sponsorship of Festivals," *Tobacco Reporter*, May 1985, p. 62.
9. Kenneth Warner, *Selling Smoke: Cigarette Advertising and Public Health* (Washington, D.C.: American Public Health Association, 1986), pp. 44-46.
10. Ronald Davis, "Current Trends in Cigarette Advertising," *New England Journal of Medicine*, Vol. 316, No. 12, 1987, p. 726.
11. "Liggett Tests a New Cigarette Developed for Hispanic Tastes," *The Wall Street Journal*, July 12, 1984, p. 33.
12. Jack Feuer, "To Segment or Not to Segment?" *Adweek*, April 11, 1988, p. 17.
13. Advertising supplement, "The Philip Morris Partnership With the Hispanic Community: A Status Report," *Hispanic Business*, September 1987, p. 28.
14. Conny Lotze, "The Latin American Spirit," *Hispanic*, March 1989, p. 61.
15. Warner, *Selling Smoke*, p. 58.
16. Coors ad, *Hispanic*, March 1988, p. 37.
17. Julie Lieblich, "If You Want a Big, New Market . . .," *Fortune*, Nov. 21, 1988, p. 184.
18. "Marketing to Hispanics: Corporate America Learns New Tricks, Revives Old Ones to Lure Latins," *The Miami Herald*, July 11, 1988.
19. Carol Wheelan, "Grassroots Efforts Grow," *Food and Beverage Marketing*, April 1987, p. 35.
20. "Hispanic Art Tour," *Hispanic Business*, January 1985, p. 31.
21. "Somerset's Hispanic Strategy," *Liquor Store*, June 1985, p. 24.

Chapter 5. Contributions to Hispanic Organizations (pages 55-74)

1. Telephone interview, March 13, 1989.
2. Telephone interview, March 12, 1989.
3. Telephone interview, March 14, 1989.
4. Personal interview, Feb. 23, 1989.

5. Telephone interview, Feb. 27, 1989.

6. Telephone interview, March 13, 1989.

7. U.S., Congress, House, Committee on Energy and Commerce, Subcommittee on Health and the Environment, *Hearings, Advertising of Tobacco Products,* 99th Cong., 2nd sess., 1986, p. 216.

8. Ibid., p. 223.

9. Telephone interview, March 16, 1989.

10. Telephone interview, March 9, 1989.

11. Telephone interview, March 15, 1989.

12. Telephone interview, March 2, 1989.

13. Personal interview, Feb. 23, 1989.

14. Telephone interview, March 15, 1989.

15. Myron Levin, "The Tobacco Industry's Strange Bedfellows," *Business and Society Review*, Spring 1988, p. 15.

16. Personal interview, Feb. 22, 1989.

17. "Chicanos Reject Beer Sponsors," *Community Resource Manager* (Sunland, Calif.), Spring 1989, Vol. 2, No. 6, p. 1.

18. Personal interview, March 2, 1989.

19. Ibid.

20. Telephone interview, March 13, 1989.

21. Personal interview, February 22, 1989.

22. Kirk Victor, "Strange Alliances," *National Journal*, Aug. 15, 1987, p. 2076.

23. Levin, "Strange Bedfellows," p. 17.

24. Victor, "Strange Alliances," p. 2077.

25. Telephone interview, March 2, 1989.

26. *Hispanic Business*, September 1987, front cover.

27. "The Hispanic Marketers: Personalities and Players," *Hispanic Business*, December 1987, p. 6.

28. *Networking: Official Newsletter of the United States Hispanic Chamber of Commerce*, 1989, pp. 2-3.

29. Telephone interview, Feb. 28, 1989.

30. "Unidos: 20 Years of Progress," program for the 20th Anniversary Conference of the National Council of La Raza, Albuquerque, N.M., July 1988.

31. Program for "1988 Training Conference and Convention," National IMAGE Inc., Cleveland, Ohio, May 24-28, 1988.

32. Brochure, "Major Sponsorship Opportunities," 1989 National Image Training Conference and Convention.

33. Telephone interview, March 9, 1989.

34. Arnoldo Torres, telephone interview, March 13, 1989.

35. Stephen Beale, "Networking the Networks," *Hispanic Business*, September 1987, p. 41.

36. "Networking," p. 1.

37. Hispanic Policy Development Project, *Windows of Opportunity: How*

Business Invests in U.S. Hispanic Markets (Washington, D.C.: Hispanic Policy Development Project, 1987), Vol. 1, p. 39.

38. "Political Education Manual," League of United Latin American Citizens, 1986.

39. JoAnn Zuniga, "One New System, Two New Pacts," *Hispanic Business*, February 1985, p. 43.

40. "In Support of the Cuban American National Council," *SER America*, Summer 1988, p. 11.

41. Conference program, "Cuban Americans in the Decade of Hispanics," Jan. 31-Feb. 2, 1988, p. 5.

42. Ibid., p. 21.

43. Brochure, "Cuban Americans in the Decade of Hispanics: The Fourth National Conference Presented by the Cuban American National Council Inc.," Jan. 31-Feb. 3, 1988.

44. "1986-1987 SER Annual Report," p. 15.

45. Annual Report, May 1987-April 1988, Mexican American Legal Defense and Educational Fund, p. 12.

46. Ibid., pp. 20-21.

47. "Ad Campaign Brewing," *Hispanic Business*, September 1986, p. 50.

48. "COSSHMO Anheuser-Busch Agreement," *Newsletter*, National IMAGE Inc., July/September 1988, p. 7.

49. Telephone interview with Jane Delgado, March 7, 1989.

50. Laton McCartney, "Cracking the Case of Coors," *Manhatten Inc.*, February 1988, p. 74

51. Chart, "Brewers' Market Share 1976-1986," *Beer Marketer's INSIGHTS*, undated.

52. Adolph Coors Company, *Annual Report 1987*, p. 29.

53. "National Agreement Between Adolph Coors Company and the Hispanic Association on Corporate Responsibility." In *The National Hispanic-Coors Agreement and the National Puerto Rican Forum: A Critique*, Institute for Puerto Rican Policy, mimeographed, March 1986.

54. Ibid.

55. Stephen Beale, "Striking a Deal with Big Business," *Hispanic Business*, February 1987, p. 30.

56. Personal interview, Feb. 23, 1989.

57. Personal interview, Feb. 22, 1989.

58. Jeff Sellers, "Golden Opportunity," *Hispanic Business*, September 1987, p. 16.

59. Calculations based on financial data from "Adolph Coors Company Annual Report 1987," pp. 28-29.

60. Personal interview, Feb. 23, 1989.

61. Telephone interview, March 9, 1989.

62. Raul Caetano, "Patterns and Problems of Drinking Among U.S. Hispanics." In *Report of the Secretary's Task Force,* Vol. VII, p. 165.

63. Rodolfo Acuna, "Put Cinco de Mayo On the Wagon," *Los Angeles Herald Examiner*, May 15, 1987, p. A21.

64. Robert Montemayor, "Cornucopia or Mirage?" *Hispanic Business*, December 1985, p. 68.

65. Personal interview, Feb. 23, 1989.

66. Tom Diaz, "Coors: Get on Board Hispanic Trend," *Nuestro*, January/February 1985, p. 14.

67. Personal interview, Feb. 23, 1989.

68. Sellers, "Golden Opportunity," p. 17.

69. Adolph Coors Company, "Caring: 1987-88 Adolph Coors Company Charitable Contributions and Donations," May 1988.

Chapter 6. Conclusions and Recommendations (pages 75-79)

1. U.S., Department of Education, Office of Educational Research and Improvement, Center for Education Statistics, "Who Drops Out of High School?" May 1987, p. 18. High-school drop-out rates: Whites, 12.2%; Blacks, 16.8%, Hispanics, 18.7%.

Index

The Center for Science in the Public Interest is a non-profit, tax-exempt organization that is concerned about the effects of technology on society. CSPI's work focuses on food, alcohol, and health. Our Alcohol Policies Project examines the marketing activities of beverage producers, taxes, labeling, and the need for comprehensive government efforts to reduce alcohol abuse and alcoholism. Both the nutrition and alcohol projects are closely linked to CSPI's Action on Minority Health project.

CSPI publishes numerous books, posters, and pamphlets for professionals, teachers, activists, and the general public. Readers of this report may be interested in several of CSPI's other publications. They include:

_____ *The Booze Merchants*, by Jacobson, Atkins, and Hacker, 161 pp., $5.95

_____ *Alcohol Warning Signs: How to Get Legislation Passed in Your City*, by Schechter, 52 pp., $4.95

_____ *Marketing Booze to Blacks*, Hacker, Collins, and Jacobson, 70 pp., $4.95

_____ *Marketing Disease to Hispanics*, by Maxwell and Jacobson, 100 pp., $6.95

_____ You are also invited to become a member of CSPI. The annual membership fee is $19.95. Members receive 10 issues of *Nutrition Action Healthletter*, a 10 percent discount on all publications, and two informative and colorful posters on food additives and nutrition.

Please indicate the number of copies of each report you would like. If you would like more information on CSPI's other activities and publications, please check here _____.

_____

(Name)

_____

(Address)

_____

(City)   (State)   (Zip)

- Make your check payable to "CSPI."
- Send this form to:

Publications
Center for Science in the Public Interest
1501 16th Street NW
Washington, DC 20036